Cancer Without Subtitles

MAIR STRATTON

DEDICATION

For Andy and Costanza
A true love and a true friend

CONTENTS

Cancer Without Subtitles

There were two things that I'd always dreaded in my life but only in that comfortable 'it'll never happen to me' way. One was getting cancer and the other was being in a hospital 'abroad'. i.e. anywhere where English isn't the first language.

I think you can guess what's coming next.

But with the added complication of a global pandemic.

It reminds me of Ginger Rogers. You remember her? Hollywood star in the 19 whatevers. Fred Astaire's dance partner. it was said that she did everything that Fred did, only backwards and in high heels.

Going through cancer in a foreign country with a foreign language was plain old ordinary cancer, only it sometimes felt like I was doing it backwards and in high heels.

I've changed all the names in here because I haven't asked anyone's permission to write about them, but all the stars of this story (and there were many) will know who they are.

Spoiler alert. The heroine survives.

Second spoiler alert. I was the heroine. It's my story so I get to play the leading role.

1 The Lump

Finding the lump, the doctor's daughter, a missing mammogram, an actual mammogram, my first ultrasound and a whole new vocabulary.

Christmas 2020

It was 9 days before Christmas when I felt the lump in my breast. We were all still in Covid lockdown and the days were long, cold and empty.

The rules in Italy were strict: going out for a drink or a meal was by now a distant memory and seeing more than 2 people outside your family circle more often than not meant shouting across a street. To leave your immediate commune you had to be either working or getting essential supplies, and you had to carry paperwork stating your reason to be outside. Not having a reason or, God forbid, lying about your reason for being out and about, was a fine of several hundred euros.

So far, I had been stopped three times by the carabinieri, which I thought was pretty average. In short, fun had become a distant memory and every TV programme worth watching had already been binge-watched.

Not surprising then that I chose to go to bed early. Normally a night owl, my horizons had shrunk so much that the idea of laying in a warm bed listening to an audio book seemed like a wild night of fun. At some stage I fell asleep and himself, as he so often did, switched off the radio when he came to bed.

I woke up needing a wee. It was pitch dark and, according to the clock, just gone 4 am. I had the usual argument with myself about just how badly I needed a wee (enough to get up in the cold and dark?) and, as usual, after ten minutes or so, my bladder won and I lost. When I returned to bed, hopping barefoot across the freezing cold floor tiles, I was tempted to tried and steal some body warmth from Himself but that seemed a bit cruel so I snuggled back into my still warm spot, wrapping my cold arms around my equally cold body.

I turned on my side and that's when I felt it. It was quite high up, in front of my armpit. A lump. Or was it? I moved my fingertips away and back again. No. There was nothing there. Or maybe there was. I felt around again, and this time I pressed down, hard. Yes, there was definitely something, but it was really deep and maybe it wasn't a lump because how were you supposed to know what a lump actually feels like? I remember a nurse, years ago, telling me I was "one of those people with naturally dense and lumpy breasts" and it was true. I've lost count of the number of times I've thought 'is this a lump or not?' and concluded it was a not.

I rolled onto my back and felt the same spot. Nothing. I rolled back onto my side and felt again. Yes, there it was. I did it twice more with the same results. I was now feeling a bit bruised because I've been pressing so hard, so I stopped and eventually went back to sleep.

When I woke up, it was the first thing I thought about. I felt around again but I was still not sure. Maybe, I thought, I'd imagined it was worse than it is. I don't know about you but, to me, everything seems like a Greek tragedy between 3am and 5am. In the shower, all soapy and slippery I held my arm up and checked again. This time it definitely felt like there was something there.

While I was drying myself, I told myself all the reasons why I was just imagining there was a lump and why I didn't need to get it checked out. I knew exactly what I was doing. I was chickening out. I carried on arguing with myself while I was dressing and then, before I could completely talk myself out of it, I grabbed my phone to text the Doctor's daughter. Breezily, deliberately making it sound like a social visit, I texted 'will you be at the surgery tomorrow? I want to ask you something'. She wrote straight back saying yes sure, come along. 'Damn', I thought, 'now I was committed'. I decided not to mention it to Himself until I knew for sure that I wasn't catastrophising. I know him. He would have started worrying and asking question after question after question and that would have made it feel way too real. Right then I was determined not to let it feel real. Plus, I had no answers.

17 December

I live in a small commune of about a thousand people in what's roughly the centre of Abruzzo, in roughly the centre of Italy. My town is typically Italian; narrow roads lined with stone houses which lead to broad open piazzas, largely empty except for special occasions. It's a mountainous area on the edge of the National Park, perfectly situated between the sea and the mountains. We are 30 minutes from the sea and roughly 40 minutes' drive from the ski lifts of the serious mountains.

The town is built on a low peak which, according to a road sign, is 369 metres above sea level. It rises steeply so that each house clinging to its edge has a spectacular view of the countryside dropping away into the distance. Just before you reach the centre and the main piazzas, the tight and winding road opens up into a broad carriageway with a stone wall shoring up the main palazzo (castle) on one side and parking spaces overlooking an open vista on the other. This was where I was headed.

Himself had already left and was in the town, at the church. A fellow member of the local choir had died unexpectedly a few days ago, so he was singing at the funeral mass. It was due to start in half an hour or so and, from the number of cars parked in the normally empty space, it seemed everyone in this small community was paying their respects. I parked in the single remaining slot and walked up to the surgery to the sombre intonation of funeral bells.

The church was in the upper piazza, just around the corner from the doctor's surgery and I could see a queue of socially distanced people outside the surgery. My heart sank. The courage I had mustered was on a strict time clock. When I got closer though, I realised they were all there for the funeral, not for the surgery. Covid restrictions at that time limited church congregations and I could see rows of white plastic chairs lined out, filling the piazza. With a half hour to go, every one had already been taken and the overflow were hovering by the surgery, chatting before the service started.

-0-

Inside the surgery no-one was waiting. The door to the dispensing room was open and I could see Cara doing something on the computer so I walked straight in. I still found the absence of formal appointment systems and receptionist barriers strange. Here, if you need to see the doctor you just turn up on surgery days and wait to be seen. So long as you memorise who is already in the waiting room you know when your turn has arrived, and just go in. This could be a peculiarity of my doctor's surgery, but I think it's actually common to most small communes; and ours is a very small commune. Cities are different of course.

Let me tell you some things about Cara that are important to know.

One. Cara isn't her real name. I'm calling her Cara for the purposes of this account.

Two. I had been helping Cara with her (already excellent) English and she had been helping me with my (just about adequate) Italian so I counted (and still count) Cara as a friend.

Three. Cara was not just the doctor's daughter but had just qualified as a doctor herself and was helping out at her father's surgery before she went onto her specialist training.

Four. Not about Cara but her father, my actual doctor. He does not speak English and whilst I'd by now revised the Italian for breast, lump and cancer (seno, nodulo, cancro[1]) I knew I might need other words I hadn't yet revised.

---

[1] Breast, lump, cancer

So you see, there was method in my madness.

Given my reluctance to even be there you probably won't be surprised that I didn't start talking about the suspect lump straight away. We chatted about the funeral and the man who had died. That took five minutes or so. Then we spent another five minutes talking about the nativity display competition, where we were in competing teams. Making a nativity display isn't something I would have ever considered in my past life but the combination of a social lockdown and a small community were persuasive incentives to get involved. Eventually I got around to mumbling that it wasn't actually a social visit and told her about the lump. She moved straight into formal doctor mode and moved me into the surgery proper where she checked my breasts and confirmed there was something there. She didn't have to tell me; I could see by the way her face went all still and concentrated that she could feel something. Damn and double damn. I had really hoped it was all my imagination.

Cara told me she would book me in for a mammogram, and that, since a lump was clearly present, I would get priority. "I must wait to hear". I went home for lunch, determined to push everything to the back of my mind. No point in worrying until I had to, I told myself, worrying myself sick. No point in sharing my anxiety. That would have made it even more real, and it was already too dangerously real for my liking.

-0-

14

After lunch I went back to the town to assemble our team's nativity entry with Himself and four of our friends. The explanation was simple. Lockdown. For six weeks or so this competition was our main entertainment and only viable excuse for ex-lockdown meet-ups so we made the most of it. In the scrubby little bit of derelict garden we had to work with we were creating a scene with the Angel Gabriel and the shepherds. With a road of hope leading to a distant stable it was all very topical but not quite as topical as he winning entry turned out to be. There was also a Christmas carol that people could play from an iPhone we fixed to the wall, and solar lights that needed installing plus it was freezing cold so we wanted to get it done as soon as possible and get warm again. It was actually a good distraction for my racing brain, and I discovered I could pretend 'all this' wasn't happening quite easily.

That lasted until we get home when I told Himself about the lump and my visit to Cara. He predictably said 'are you sure?' predictably followed by 'why didn't you tell me?' I answered 'yes I was sure' (thinking 'no of course I'm not sodding sure I'm just making it up as a joke what do you think?') and 'I'm telling you now' (thinking 'and I wished I hadn't because now you're worrying too'). Later that afternoon though, Cara appeared at the house clutching a piece of paper for me so I was glad I had. It was my appointment at Chieti hospital for a mammogram and ultrasound at the beginning of the next week. That would have been a bit tricky to explain away.

-0-

The next day I began panicking about the language problem. What if I couldn't understand what people were saying to me? it was not like it hasn't ever happened before. It happened and still happens daily. I hesitated long and hard, then sent a text to my just had an operation herself and really should be at home recovering friend Cristina, in the hope that she would come with me and be my translator. She said no. Not because she didn't want to but, as she reminded me, because there was a pandemic going on and "did you forget we're living in a red zone?". Yes I had. I had also forgotten that even her husband wasn't allowed into the hospital when she had her operation. In short, the chances of me having a friend to hold my hand while I had a few straightforward tests were less than zero. I was on my own.

22 December

Three days before Christmas and six o'clock in the morning we got out of bed and prepared to drive to Chieti hospital. It was earlier than I'd have liked but if I was honest, anxiety woke me up anyway. It was also much earlier than we needed. The appointment was for 9am and we were sitting in the hospital car park by 8.15. Normally I'd had given Himself an earful about his insistence on being early for everything but this time I was on his side.

By 8.30 I couldn't take the suspense anymore and decided to go in. As I walked to the entrance I realised I was actually physically shaking with nerves. It wasn't because of the mammogram (I already knew how horrible that would be) but fear of the unknown and my ability to navigate it. I'd never been in Chieti hospital, or any Italian hospital and had no idea how the Italian system worked. Where should I go? Would I be able to find the right place? What was the protocol? What if I couldn't understand anybody? What if they couldn't understand me?

There was a security guard at the entrance, taking everyone's temperature before they were allowed to enter, checking that masks were adequate and watching to be sure hands were disinfected. I said a shaky buon giorno which he ignored, just jerking his head to say I could go though. I thanked him. I didn't need to, but I was sort of testing my voice out to make sure it didn't sound as wobbly as I felt. Inside, my nerves doubled. I'd just come in on the ground floor, my papers said I needed to be on Floor 5, but the signs told me I was on Floor 7. This couldn't possibly be right. I went back to ask the security guard who wasn't best pleased to see me walking the wrong way in his one-way system. He wasn't exactly rude, but he told me it wasn't his job. It's worth noting that "not my job mate" is remarkably easy to translate as the body language is identical in both languages. As he obviously wasn't about to help me, I went back inside to find the information desk.

Information was at the far end of the reception area and the woman at the desk was far more helpful. In fact, in response to my careful "Excuse me, could you tell me where I need to go for a mammogram?" she gave me a veritable torrent of instructions. Unfortunately, because she was behind a glass screen, wearing a mask and speaking in Italian that was faster than the speed of light, I was completely lost after about the fourth word. My nervousness ratcheted up several notches.

I followed what I hoped were her instructions and ended up in roughly the right place, wandering around the radiology department, where I saw someone in green scrubs and asked directions again. This time I asked them to speak slowly, and they did. Well, not slowly exactly, but slowly enough so that it wasn't a blur of sound. It seemed I had to check in first, but I had to wait until my appointment time before I could do it. They pointed me to the unmanned Radiology check in office which I had already walked through once, so I went back, sat down on one of the chairs that wasn't taped off and watched the clock until 9am and the staff arrived.

Checking in was actually remarkably easy because I just mumbled that I had an appointment and shoved my paperwork across the counter. They processed it then sent me round the corner to a corridor where the screening rooms were, telling me to wait to be called into room 7. I sat in the deserted corridor and tried to read the multiple notices taped to the doors. They mainly concerned Covid regulations, reminding people that only physically disabled people could be accompanied and I thought it was a bit unfair that lack of language wasn't classed as an actual disability. On the plus side I learned one new word while I was waiting – spogliatoio which my word reference dictionary told me was Italian for changing room. It wasn't long before I had that word off pat.

After a while, just as the anxiety was climbing from my stomach into my chest, I was called in. There were two medical staff. "Had I had a mammogram before?" one of them asked.

"Yes".

"When?"

"A couple of years ago".

"Ok, good. Show it to me".

"I can't, I don't have a copy of it".

They frowned and muttered at each other, then tried again.

"We need to see your last mammogram" the female doctor said, very slowly and distinctly. They clearly thought I hadn't understood the question. "You must show it to us."

I explained that, in England, you just get told the result of your mammogram in a letter. It's just positive or negative. You don't get to keep or even see your mammogram films. There was a lot more frowning and muttering and I was fairly sure they didn't believe me, but in the end they shrugged their collective shoulders in a fabulously resigned manner and said "Okay. You don't have it so we start from scratch".

The man told me to go into the spogliatoio and strip off (I thought 'good job I just learned that word') then it was mammogram time. If you have ever had a mammogram, I can tell you that it is just as horrible in Italy as it is in the UK. If you haven't, then I don't have the words to tell you how horrible they are. Suffice to say, mammogram machines must had been invented by men and those men should had had their own precious testicles squashed flat between two bits of heavy metal before they decided it was the best design.

After my poor breasts had been thoroughly mangled, I went into a second room with two other people who laid me on a gurney to do an ultrasound. I had only ever had one of these before so it was quite interesting if a little squelchy. It took about 20 minutes and there was a lot of discussion in very fast Italian that, in the main, I couldn't follow. At one point they asked me to slide myself down. By the time I had processed and translated the words, everyone had stopped what they were doing to look at me. Embarrassed, I committed the words to memory along with get undressed and changing room. Good job I did. They all turned out to be words I needed quite a lot in the future.

Ultrasound finished I was dried off with copious handfuls of white paper towels, sent to dress again, then told to wait outside. This time there were two other people in the corridor, so I selected a seat suitably distant and began reading the notices again. I made a note to bring a kindle if I needed to do this again, being still optimistic that this might be my first and last hospital visit.

Ha! How foolish was I? The brief burst of optimism didn't last long.

About twenty minutes later the male doctor emerged holding a typed report on my procedures and a CD of both the ultrasound and mammogram. When he made a big point of telling me that I had to keep these to show in future I was sure beyond doubt that they hadn't believed me about the English system. I didn't really care though, because he told me something much worrying. He told me that the lump was suspect. Not only that, it was "brutto e profondo" (ugly and deep) and I that I would have to have a biopsy. They would call me with a date. It would most likely be "after the holidays". If I was nervous when I came in, now I was terrified.

Christmas Day

I don't remember Christmas Day. I can remember the Christmas before and the Christmas before that and the Christmas before that, but I have absolutely no recollection of this Christmas. I suspect I spent a lot of it inside myself.

2 The Biopsy

The biopsy, brutto e profondo, a New Year meltdown, problems with the health card and a formal diagnosis.

December 29th

It was 4 days after Christmas and I woke up dreading the phone call, as I had done every day since Boxing Day. I remembered the date and relaxed a little. So close to the New Year I could safely assume the call would be coming in January and I had a reprieve. It gave me a chance to do something positive and get my Tessera Sanitaria sorted out.

The Tessera Sanitaria is like the UK's National Health card, registering you with a GP and entitling you to medical treatment. It means that most treatments and medicines are either free or discounted and it is not automatic for non-citizens unless you are either employed in Italy or a pensioner formally resident in the country. As I was (am) neither I instead make an annual voluntary payment for my Tessera Sanitaria. It is a quirk of the system that the card can only be purchased in a lump sum and it is only ever valid to the 31st of December each year.

The fee is the same regardless of whether you buy the card in January or November, so it makes sense to get it as early in January as possible. Given what was happening it was vital that I got mine renewed as soon as I could.

It wasn't yet January but we hoped we might be able to renew our cards a bit early; unlikely, but worth a shot. With this in mind we went to the ASL office at Llama Dei Peligni. It was a waste of time. When we got to the office it was closed until January.

December 30th

I was wrong about getting the phone call in January.

On any other December 30th I would have been up early, preparing for a New Year's Eve party. Instead, with all our plans kyboshed by Covid, I was still lying in my warm bed when my mobile rang. Completely relaxed I reached over and answered it.

"Pronto"

"Signora Stratton? Sto chiamando dall'ospedale…."

Eek! As soon as I heard the word "ospedale" I scrambled naked out of bed and ran into the kitchen, shouting "aspetta, aspetta" (wait, wait) into the phone. Scrabbling for a pen and a scrap of paper I saw a pair of curious eyes watching me through the window. Fortunately, it was just one of the cats.

"Ok" I panted "I'm ready now".

'8am tomorrow' I wrote.

'Floor 5' I wrote.

'Need a ricetta' (prescription) I wrote.

When I ended the call I was shaking and I wasn't sure if it was the cold of the kitchen or because I was so frightened. I think it was a bit of both.

I found Himself and told him then called Cara who said she would sort the ricetta out and drop it round later. In the end she got stuck in another surgery so it was her father (my actual doctor) who drove half an hour to Lama dei Peligni to get my ricetta rushed through and then put it in our mailbox at 8pm. Cara texted me to tell me it was there and that he had also paid the fee for me. I was not to worry. I could pay him back later. Good luck tomorrow she said.

New Year's Eve

We got up at 5.30am which is a god-forsaken time of the morning in the summer let alone the midst of winter. Once again we were too early, arriving at the hospital by 7.30am but I was far too antsy to wait in the car so I went straight in. The security guard checked me over, allowed me through and this time I went straight to floor 7, 2 floors down, and Radiology's empty reception area. It was 7.35am and radiology didn't open until 8 so I plopped myself into a plastic chair and opened my kindle. While I pretended to read I was anxiously watching other people arrive and worrying about being pushed to the back of the queue.

At ten minutes to eight I cracked and abandoned my chair to hover carelessly by the desk, like I wasn't really worried about queue jumpers but I just needed to stretch my legs. The instant the woman opened the window I was there and, without saying anything over and above the obligatory Buon Giorno, I handed her my ricetta.

Something was not right. She pushed it back at me, with a blast of way too fast to follow Italian. This was when I realised beyond doubt that the combination of rapid Italian plus face mask plus glass screens was going to a recurring problem[2].

I pushed it back at her, saying "I've an appointment for a biopsy, and it's for right now". She called over a colleague. He called over another colleague. They huddled together and passed the ricetta back and forth amongst them, sounding agitated. This didn't mean anything of course. If you spend any time in Italy you soon realise that Italians can made a lullaby sound agitated. Hands were waved. Fingers were pointed. Voices were raised. Then the original woman came back to the window and fired a question at me that I didn't understand because I was by now too stressed to even try to follow what she was saying. Instead, I just shoved my whole file through the aperture. They all pored over it and a fourth person joined the discussion. This person seems to have had some sway because the woman handed me my file back and told me I could go through. 'Where?' I asked and she sent me through to the same corridor as before.

---

[2] I was right. It never got easier.

I didn't wait long this time. Almost immediately I was taken straight into the second room of my first visit, where the ultrasound had been done. I sat at a desk diagonally adjacent to the doctor, an attractive blonde woman with long hair in a bun, and answered a series of questions before signing several consent forms. I didn't have a clue what I was consenting to, but it was safe to assume that nothing would be happening until I signed, so I did. Determined to understand as much as I could, I asked several times for things to be repeated more slowly and everyone was very patient with me. The attractive doctor, who seemed to be in overall charge, finally explained, clearly and slowly, what the process would be, then sent me to the changing room to take my top clothes off.

I thought I'd be scared at this point but actually I was quite relieved that we were getting to the actual biopsy because, by then, I just wanted it over with.

When I returned, stripped to the waist, I had to lay on a gurney, turned onto my side facing the wall, with my right arm lifted over my head. The wall had a three dimensional paper sculpture on it, like a red and pink flower and I wondered if it was significant. I thought maybe it was a cancer symbol or maybe somebody who worked there just liked origami. Either way I didn't like it very much.

One nurse put a tourniquet on my left arm and inserted a canula into my inside elbow. This wasn't, in the end, used for anything so I assume it was a precaution. My right arm was lifted more firmly over my head and I was injected with a local anaesthetic.

By this stage there were 5 people in the room with me, and they stayed there throughout.

The actual process of the biopsy took an hour. It hurt a bit but in a pushy tuggy so of way, easily borne and more like a really hard pressure rather than any sharp pain. To me, the whole process felt weird: very caring yet at the same time completely impersonal. The doctors I couldn't see were talking about me as if I were nothing more than my dodgy breast and the nurses I could see touched my hand and raised their eyebrows in an 'are you alright?' question every time we made eye contact. Every so often the doctors out of sight would stop and ask if I was okay too. At one stage I did feel a burning sensation but as soon as I mentioned it, they did something that stopped it immediately, presumably by pumping in more anaesthetic.

I tried really hard to understand what was being said but I was facing away from the surgeons, looking at the paper sculpture on the wall and it was too fast and conversational for me to follow. Nonetheless I could tell they were not happy and I thought I heard two of them agreeing that there was 'something there'.

I was right. When it was over and I was sitting up the blonde doctor confirmed it. She told me there was definitely 'something there'. The words 'brutto e profondo' were mentioned again and I noticed how much the rolled r's in Italian (Brrrrutto, Prrrofondo) made brutto and profondo sound so much worse than a simple ugly and deep. Although ugly and deep sounded pretty grim too.

While I was still absorbing the horrible reality of my lump she told me that they would consult with their colleagues in Ortona, which was the regional cancer centre, and contact me again within two weeks.

-0-

By 10am I was back in the corridor, with an ice pack tucked inside my bra, waiting for my report. I opened my kindle to read while I was waiting and got through several chapters, although I still have no idea what I actually read. Eventually, 45 minutes later, the door opened and the chap I'd labelled doctor 2 handed me another small folder with my latest results. He reminded me that I had to keep them safe and told me that I now had to go back to the reception desk and pay the fee.

I hadn't realised there was a fee to pay. Maybe that's what the earlier problem was. Either way, I didn't (and still don't) mind paying a fee. In fact, I was glad to. In Italy it is usual to pay a fee towards the cost of any tests or procedures you have, even with the Tessera Sanitaria. It is not the full cost but if you don't turn up or cancel in plenty of time you are charged the full fee. I think having to pay a full fee for appointments you miss without cancelling is a good idea and something they should introduce in the UK. In this case, the fee was 36 euros. That's over and above the money that I owed to my doctor but even so, it didn't seem enough for what had just happened.

I mentally added up the cost of the number of staff and the equipment and the three hours I was in there and reckoned the real cost must be enormous. I wondered how much it was. I wondered what the system was in other European counties. I wondered how Americans cope when they get ill. I wondered why so many Americans support the idea of a privatised medicine when it is so obviously not in their interest. I deliberately wondered about all these things because it stopped me thinking about what she'd told me. "Brutto. Profondo. Non è buono".

I walked back to the car park holding my folder with my latest report inside, trying desperately hard not to cry. It worked until I saw Himself waiting for me. He was standing outside the car despite the freezing cold and looked frozen. He had clearly been there a while. My eyes filled with tears and my bottom lip wobbled. He opened his arms and pulled me into a hug and the tears spilled over. Somehow I stammered out what I had just been told and we both snivelled for a while before we pulled ourselves together enough to get in the car.

-0-

All the bars were shut so we couldn't even go somewhere for a coffee to talk about it. Instead, we talked about it as he drove home. "Whatever it is", he said, "we just have to get through it and we'll do it together". Then he explained to me in some detail the process I've been through and the significance of lymph nodes. I realised I wasn't the only one who had been secretly reading every bit of breast cancer information I could get my hands on.

Halfway home we distracted ourselves by going to a big supermarket. I know that sounds dull but we only had a tiny supermarket in our commune so this one - off limits to us in a red zone lockdown – was a real treat. After all, there's no point in having a medical permission to be on the roads and not using it to the full. In fact, it would have been a sin.

29

In a daze of greed and grief we decided to make ourselves a really, really special New Year's Day meal and bought lots of expensive foods and edible treats. It briefly – very briefly – made me feel better.

-0-

Once home I wrote to my Italian friend of mammogram request fame and told her what had happened. Also to Cara who replied telling me to be positive. I said I was okay (even though I wasn't) and that I knew I'd be fine because I'd seen lots of people go through it and held their hands so I knew what to expect. She replied again saying she would be with me to hold my hand. So I cried another little bit.

New Year's Day

It was New Year's Day and the happy new year messages that flooded in all morning seemed like a very bad joke to me. Naturally, I still replied to them all and even sent my own in-between preparing yesterday's extravagant foods to cook later. If anything, I was a little bit smug about how well I was holding it together, especially when the only two guests we were allowed for the day arrived. I told myself that nobody could possibly have guessed anything was wrong as we waded through excessive quantities of alcohol and finger foods. Later, when we finally told people, I knew I was right.

Eventually of course they left and we were alone again. Still, everything was fine as we cooked together and carried on drinking. Alcohol. That was the mistake. If you want to destroy your emotional defences alcohol is probably the best weapon you have. We had only just managed to eat the first part of our special New Year's Day meal when everything welled up, overflowed and, out of nowhere, I started to bawl. Himself pulled me from the table and onto the settee and wrapped me in his arms while I sobbed and sobbed and sobbed. God knew how long for. It was my second total meltdown since I found the lump. The expensive and carefully cooked dinner never got eaten.

January 3rd

I spoke to my mum in the UK. She said, thinking of Covid "I can't say happy new year because none of us can say that now instead I'll wish you a healthy new year".

I said nothing. I might had snivelled a bit afterwards though.

January 4th

January 4th meant the ASL office in Lama Dei Peligni was open again. Getting my Tessera Sanitaria renewed was by now urgent, so we went there as a priority, paid the annual fee at the Post Office and took the proof of payment to the office administrator. This being her first day back she had a mountain of work on her desk and a queue of people waiting to see her, so we left everything with her. She promised to call as soon as it was processed.

January 12th

It was 12 days after the biopsy and I was still in bed (8am) when my phone rang[3]. I recognised the number as the hospital in Chieti, leapt out of bed and ran into the kitchen to take the

---

[3] In bed AGAIN. I know, I know. But it was winter and it was cold and we were in lockdown.

call. I've no idea why I ran into the kitchen each time I got a scary call. It just seemed important to be upright.

A woman told me the results were ready and I panicked, thinking she was about to tell me the results over the phone. My ears stopped functioning completely and my brain froze; this was too important to me to blag my way through translation; what if I misunderstood? Anyway I wasn't ready. I stopped her before she could say anything more, gabbling that I wanted her to call Cristina's number instead, and that Cristina would translate for me. After a pause she agreed and let me give her Cristina's number. I told her then slumped onto a high stool and shook for a few seconds before remembering I needed to prewarn Cristina.

I called Cristina but her phone was engaged so I redialled and then again. When I finally got through Cristina told me that they'd already phoned. I took a deep, shaky breath then let it out as Cristina added that she didn't have my results; they'd just been calling to tell me that I had to go to the hospital and pick up my biopsy results before 1pm. Today. That's something else that's different about the Health Service here, and something I quickly got used to. There are no letters setting appointments weeks in advance: it is all phone calls telling you to 'be here tomorrow', or in this case today. I still wonder how people who have proper jobs with proper fixed hours manage.

Himself drove me to Chieti again. He needed to be useful. and I was in no emotional state to concentrate so it made sense.

32

He waited in the car and I went inside to wait, alone, outside the consulting room where I had the biopsy. When I was called in it was the same (male) doctor who did my original ultrasound, and the same (female) doctor who did the biopsy. There was no beating about the bush. I was still standing up as she told me that the cancer diagnosis she suspected had been confirmed. "But the good thing" she added quickly, "is that it hasn't spread to your lymph nodes".

'So what's next?' I asked, and she told me.

I followed her quite well until she mentioned sending a fax which completely threw me; partly because it was years since I had heard of someone sending faxes and partly because she seemed to be asking me something about the fax. What fax? Was I supposed to be sending this fax? How could I send a fax? I held my hand up for a pause and asked her to repeat the last part again. She got flustered thinking I hadn't understood at all and tried to explain everything again in English. This was actually a lot worse than telling me in Italian and I stopped her again, saying it was just the last part I hadn't quite got.

Somehow, in a muddled mishmash of English and Italian we managed to establish that I had in fact understood properly: there was a fax involved but she was asking me if I wanted her to send a fax to Ortona to get me into treatment. "OF COURSE I want to get into treatment!" I shouted "I've got bloody cancer. Why wouldn't I want to get into treatment? Actually that's a lie. I was shouting inside but on the outside I didn't say that at all. I just very politely said "Yes please, if you could send a fax that would be great. You don't need to ask me."

More explanations followed. She was asking me because, apparently, I had the option of saying no to Ortona. If I wanted to be treated somewhere else, like Milan for example, I could choose to go there instead. I reassured her that I was happy with Ortona. Cara had told me that it was a regional centre of excellence and besides, the last place I wanted to be treated was in a strange city far from home. So far as I was concerned Ortona was already quite far away and quite unknown enough.

I was given a sheet of paper confirming the diagnosis which I added to my file and told to expect a call from the hospital in Ortona. I walked out crying but at the same time feeling better than I had done since the day I found the lump. I was strangely relieved – almost euphoric. Yes, I definitely had cancer but having the diagnosis meant that we/ I could get on with fixing it.

Himself was outside the car again when I got to the car park – too stressed to sit still - and came to meet me. I told him it was cancer but that it hadn't spread, so now both of us were crying. Fear? Relief? A bit of both but more the second. On the way home – this being the first week in the more relaxed yellow zone, we stopped at Guardiagrele and had lunch out to celebrate.

January 13th

Having heard nothing about the Tessera Sanitaria we drove over to Lama to chase it up. Chasing things up is, in my view, always better done in person, especially when you are a troublesome English person. It took us 3 years of unsuccessfully trying before we got our first Tessera Sanitaria and the administrator at Lama Dei Peligni, a lovely lady called

Celeste, was the one who finally fixed it for us. I had absolute faith in her, so her grimace as we walked in was not a good sign. It seemed like there was a problem, she told us. It was something to do with Brexit. Because of Brexit she has been told she can't process the new cards. She shrugged apologetically. "Apparently", she told us, "it's not possible".

This was my worst nightmare but after the disaster of Brexit I had prepared myself for these sorts of situations and had my 'Everything To Prove I Am Legitimately Resident' file with me. I pulled out the Attestazione and showed it to her, along with a print-out from a government website explaining how the Attestazione worked, and how it proved we, as residents, still had all the same rights[4] as we had had pre-Brexit.

She studied it and made a phone call to the powers that be, but the person at the other end of the line wasn't impressed. She shook her head as she put the phone down, saying she would take photocopies of our attestazione and to leave it with her. I asked when the cards would be ready and she shrugged again, saying she wasn't sure. We would have to wait to see if she could process them or not. It would be a week before she could tell us anything about success or otherwise. It may be that it just wasn't possible.

At this point I stopped being calm and reasonable and burst into tears, wailing I that I had cancer and had to go to the hospital. Celeste was horrified. Himself took over and explained the situation to her more calmly. Over my snotty-faced snivelling head that was by now buried in his shoulder, he reiterated the importance of the Attestazione and pleaded

---

[4] Not all the same rights unfortunately, but the same rights so far as health care was concerned.

with her to please try. She promised to do whatever she could, and we believed her.

Back in the car I wiped away the tell-tale mascara smeared under my eyes and plastered a smile on so we could meet our friends and team-mates of nativity project fame. It was time to celebrate our non-victory with a very boozy and jolly lunch.

-0-

The very next day Celeste called. She told us to come in, bringing our passports. We went there and, yes, against all odds she not just had fixed it, but fixed it in record time. She gave us paper copies of our new Tessera Sanitaria there and then. I could had hugged her but thanks to Covid, I didn't. Instead, Himself took her a plant (the flower shops had also been closed by Covid) to say thank you the next day.

-0-

Until now all this was known only to me, Himself Cara and Cristina. And Celeste of course, but she's a relative stranger. I'd decided not to tell anyone anything until I knew what I was dealing with. To be honest, at this point I still didn't know what I was dealing with, but we had gone beyond the stage of pretending it wasn't happening so the next hurdle was going public.

It was time to talk to someone else. More specifically, someone that I knew had been through it herself. Twice. So it was that poor Susan, thinking she was going out for a pleasant Covid-permitted walk and a gossipy chat got hit with my news. Once she got past the 'why didn't you said anything' routine that I was to become horribly familiar with, she was brilliantly reassuring. It made a real difference talking to someone with experience of the same thing, even if it was a few years ago and in the UK.

3 Waiting

**A missed call or five, getting an Esenzione
and Thumper gets involved.**

January 15ᵗʰ to January 27ᵗʰ

By Tuesday of the following week I was starting to worry that I
still hadn't heard from the hospital in Ortona. I thought maybe
I was being unreasonable (it was only four days after all) so I
asked Cara what she thought. She said that if there was no
news by the end of the week I should tell her and she would
chase it. She apologised for not being totally available to me. I
couldn't believe that she was apologising: this was the woman
who had sent me personal texts to keep my spirits up and
dropped everything, running around out of hours to help me
when I needed it. This was also the woman who was working
in the regional Covid Health Team as well as in the local
surgery and had told me that everything was so horrible, she
was working so hard and the hours were so long and she felt
so helpless that she sometimes just wanted to cry and cry.

Two days later, on the Thursday, Cristina called me and told me to come to the ASL in Lama ("now") because she had just spoken to Celeste about me having an Esenzione. I'd vaguely heard of an Esenzione. but had no idea what it was, so I asked. Turns out it is a special pass that that is given to pensioners and the gravely compromised ("that means you now") to provide payment exemption for medical tests. I actually thought the cost of the tests I had had so far were a real bargain, but this was a gift horse, and I wasn't about to look in it's mouth. I went to Lama, met Cristina and showed Celeste my diagnosis letter. She copied it for proof, gave me my own Esenzione and told me to be sure to take it with me when I went to Ortona. "Good luck" she said, "I hope everything goes well'.

By Friday there was still nothing from Ortona so I told Cara. She passed the problem over to her father, (Doctor) Thumper.

Thumper (we leave the Doctor part off) isn't really called Thumper. We affectionately call him that because, in our experience, whatever problem you present him with is tested with a firm poke.

When I went to see him with an ear infection he poked my ear so hard I had to be scraped off the surgery ceiling. When I fell down some steps and had a massive haematoma form on my leg, he came to the house and poked my thigh really hard. My ceiling at home is higher but I still hit it. He said it was to establish that my leg wasn't broken, but he could have just asked. When an English friend visiting had a stomach problem so bad she couldn't crawl out of bed, I called him for help. Although she is not a patient or a resident he made a home visit and poked her in the stomach. She hit the ceiling and fell back into the bed where he injected her with some magic potion. It cleared the problem within hours. We absolutely love Thumper but kind of dread seeing him all at the same time.

Anyway, Thumper called Ortona Hospital to find out why they hadn't called me and this is where it got embarrassing. Apparently I had been phoned, more than once, but I didn't answer the call. Of course I denied this vociferously but when I investigated further I realised it was true. Ortona hospital uses a Pescara telephone code instead of the Ortona code I'd been expecting. I'd actually received and dismissed several calls from a Pescara code, thinking they were just nuisance calls. Worse than that, their first call to me was on the same day they gave me the diagnosis There was I complaining about the delay, and there were they moving me on to the next stage within hours. Thumper said they would call me again the next day and I promised on my life (literally) to answer it this time.

I hovered over my phone all the next day but when I'd heard nothing by the end of it Cara said she would chase again. I told her I would take any date at any time. One day later she called me back saying they had tried to call me, several times, but without success. Not to worry though, because I had an appointment for the following Friday.

As soon as I finished the call with Cara, I checked my phone for missed calls. There were none. Lying bastards I thought.

I was soon proved wrong. That same afternoon the doctor in Chieti who had done my ultrasound also called me. He was calling on behalf of Ortona because 'the people there hadn't been able to get hold of me[5] and were getting anxious about my treatment. They thought I maybe hadn't understood that I needed to do this as soon as possible'. Because he'd spoken with me before, they'd asked him to explain the urgency to me.

I apologised, said there'd been some sort of problem but I was fixed up now. He wished me luck.

-0-

While I was waiting for Friday I looked up the hospital on the web. It looked to be about an hours' drive away and various sites gave different floors for senology. I had a choice of floor 3, floor 5 or floor 4. That wasn't good. But at least they all agreed on the address so we could plan the route there. I downloaded and translated all the information I could find about the hospital and also made myself a little cancer dictionary in Italian, hoping this would let me recognise words. I also bought myself a folder to put all of my scans and appointment and letters in and labelled it carefully. Each time I had been to the hospital I'd seen people walking around with identical folders and now I knew why. Mine started as quite a slim folder but very soon fattened up as I added plastic files inside to separate the contents into subject headings. As I write this it's now so fat and battered I need to buy something more

[5] That was when discovered that I hadn't just dismissed the Pescara number (aka Ortona hospital) as being a nuisance call. I had actually blocked the number completely.

41

robust.

4 TESTING TIMES

A fierce reception(ist), guessing games, the first oncology consultation, another ultrasound, confusing bra sizes and a blood emergency.

January 29th

We drove to Ortona to find the hospital which, as predicted, took just over an hour. When we walked in (stopped for temperature check, stopped to disinfect hands) we immediately spotted the big board listing all the departments and scooted over to find senology. Bummer. Turned out senology was on 3 floors after all, depending on what treatment you needed. Slightly panicking even though I was in plenty of time I showed the woman on reception my bits of paper and she told me I needed to go to floor 3. She smiled at me warmly. Then she turned to Himself standing silently and supportively by my side and snarled "Not you. You can't go!".

A bit taken aback by her ferocity we both recoiled in unison. it was easy to forget just how seriously Covid was[6] taken in Italy. It didn't matter because we'd already agreed he'd

---

[6] At the time of writing (January 2022) it still is.

drive to a nearby winery for restocking vital supplies while I was doing my stuff, but it was still a bit of a blow.

We bumped face masks, he left, and I went through the doors into the main hospital. The stairs took me to the third floor where I came out into a long-tiled corridor and a choice of turning left or right. With no real clues for the right direction, I dithered and chose the left hand side. The left had what looked like a large waiting room at the end, the right had lots of closed doors. It was the right choice so I went inside and joined the people already waiting. There were not that many of them and they were all socially distanced sitting in separated seats or standing ostentatiously by an open window breathing in "fresh air". I'll say it was fresh – it was bloody freezing outside.

There was a desk that looked like it might be for reception so I hung around beside that for a while. Nobody came. I thought of asking one of the other patients but nobody looked approachable. They all looked like me, internally focused and silent. Apart for the subdued ripple of obligatory Buon Giornos as I walked in, nobody had said anything. Eventually, feeling a bit foolish hovering by a desk that was so clearly unused I went and peered along the two corridors that led off the room, one to each side. The right-hand corridor had a sign saying secretary a short distance along it, so I went and knocked on the open door. I didn't ask if I was in the right place but told the gaggle of nurses inside that I had an appointment and gave them my name. Thankfully I was in the right place and it was exactly the right thing to do. I was given a ticket (like in a supermarket deli queue; number 68) and told to wait until I was called.

CANCER WITHOUT SUBTITLES

-0-

Back in the sterile waiting room I watched the other patients and tried to diagnose them. (Had I known at the time that everyone in this particular waiting room had breast cancer it would have made it a bit easier). Most of them looked perfectly normal, not like cancer patients at all. This surprised me because, even though I knew better, I still half expected to be in a room full of gaunt people. Not only did everyone look normal but as time went on there were an awful lot of them. It was a revelation to me just how many people were walking around anonymously with cancer, which I guess is something every cancer patient has to discover for himself.

Good as this game was it didn't really sustain my interest for the half an hour I was there beyond my scheduled appointment time. I looked around and wondered who chose pale lemon for the walls, and why. I wondered why Italian hospitals are so fond of crucifixes. I also wondered why there were memorial plaques to doctors in the waiting room. It seemed kind of nice but disturbing all at the same time.

I stopped wondering about the decor and started timing people as they went in and out. I concluded they were there for radiotherapy as they were all ten minutes or less. Like most of my early assumptions this was completely wrong; there is no radiotherapy at Ortona. Only two people disappeared for a long time and I thought they must be at the same stage as me and still being investigated. Twice I jumped up thinking it was my turn (nerves). Finally, I was called.

Following a nurse, I went along the right-hand corridor again and into a consulting room on the left. Inside, a nurse (doctor? I don't know) asked me a ton of questions, entering my answers into a computer. I had Google Translate on my phone all ready to go but only had to revert to it once. Now, I can't remember what the word I needed was, but it completely stumped me at the time. When we finished, she sent me outside to another, smaller waiting room diagonally opposite the consulting room.

All waiting rooms are soulless but this one was my worst. It was a small, oblong room, painted in virulent pink, with chairs along three walls and a bookcase and low table against the other. It was empty of people so, desperate for distraction after just 5 minutes, I examined the books. Of course, they were all in Italian. I picked up one by an American author I recognised, and tried to translate the synopsis but my heart wasn't in it. There was a stack of paper and several containers full of crayons on the table, clearly meant for children. I was tempted but left them alone and sat staring into space instead.

5 or 10 minutes later, again called back into the consulting room, I stripped off for an ultrasound. A new doctor asked me questions as he stared into the computer.

He slid and pressed. "Have you had any discharge?"

"No" I replied.

Slide, slide, press again. What's your bra size?

"In Italian? I haven't a clue".

I wanted to ask him why my bra size was relevant but I my brain wouldn't think of the right Italian words. There were a lot of questions I wanted to ask and didn't during this whole process. More often than not, by the time I'd worked out what I wanted to say, the opportunity had passed. I tried to make sure I asked all the important questions but the ones that fell into the category of 'stuff that isn't vital but I'd quite like to know the answer anyway' got jettisoned very early on.

After I was dressed again we sat at the desk for some more questions and exchanging of documents. The Tessera Sanitaria was essential and they also asked for the Esenzione. The nurse/doctor (who was very clear and whose Italian I could follow) told me I would have to go for an MRI scan in Chieti and booked me in for the following Wednesday at 8am. I would also have to had blood tests and take certain pills (they gave me a list and a schedule) before the exam, so I needed to get a prescription from my doctor. More paper was handed over and I left.

-0-

Once outside I felt slightly shell shocked, but not so much that we didn't take full advantage of our Covid travel permission to shop at a big supermarket on the way home. We bought snacky things for the evening because friends were coming over for extended early evening drinks. Before they arrived I sent a text to Cara telling her I now needed a scan and she said she would come and see me on Sunday.

-0-

Sunday arrived and Cara called me to say she would come over at 5pm but needed to sleep first. Knowing that she had done seven 12-hour COVID-19 shifts that week I replied she could come whenever she wanted and reiterated how much I appreciated her help. Mentally, I thought 5pm plus tiredness meant at least 6 to 6.30 then factor in Italian time and we were looking at 7.30 or 8 before she got to me. When her car pulled up outside it was only about 6.15 so she was ridiculously early.

Cara went through everything with me and to my ABSOLUTE HORROR I discovered that I needed to have both the blood tests and the results before the scan on Wednesday. Worse, you had to make an appointment to get a blood test and the results would take 48 hours. Plus, the clinic at Lama De Peligni only did blood tests them on Tuesdays and Thursdays. It was now Sunday so I was, as they say, well stuffed. Cara helpfully pointed out that I could easily have gone to the local hospital at Casoli to get them, but now it was too late there too. I really didn't need to hear that right then. But she redeemed herself by making a phone call to the district nurse. This was the first time I realised that there was such a thing in Italy.

I listened as she did it. ("Sorry to call you on a Sunday night ....."). At the end she told me it was fixed. A woman called Annette would be coming to the house at 8am the next morning to take my blood. She gave me Annette's number and then offered to come to the MRI scan with me as she had a rare day off that day. I knew she had much better things to do on her day off than hold my hand, but I had no shame in accepting her offer instantly.

#

The following morning I was up and ready by 8am but nobody came. At 9ish I called Annette's number and left what I hoped wasn't too garbled a message. At 10ish I sent a text to Cara. Cara replied within 10 minutes saying she had spoken to

Annette and there was a misunderstanding. Annette would actually be coming the next day at 8am and she would give me my results on Tuesday afternoon.

Himself and I went to the commune and booked into the commune's COVID-19 screening for next Saturday.

#

Blood test, round two. This time I was up and showered and ready for the nurse by 7.30. No sign of the Nurse at 8.00 but at 8.05 she called me – she was by the church - where do I live? I gave her directions and she was with me 3 minutes later.

Annette was maybe mid 40s, very attractive and very efficient. By 8.15 a bucket of blood (well a large ampoule) had been taken from my arm and I was pressing a pad onto my inner elbow which she then taped in place. I confirmed with her that I would be getting the results back that day because I needed them for a scan tomorrow and she said "Yes but…"

But? BUT? I really didn't want to hear any sentence with 'but' in it.

"But" she continued, "there is a problem because the computers at Lama Dei Peligni are down. So I will go to Casoli instead and let's hope".

I didn't want to hope, but I didn't have any choice. We chit chatted as she was packing up to leave and she admired my Chinese warrior then - just as she was walking out of the door - I remembered that I was supposed to pay her. Annette waved her hand at me, "do not worry yourself – you can pay me when I bring me the results".

-0-

That afternoon Himself decided that we deserved a trip out so, given that the bars would close at 6pm (yellow zone restriction) we left the house at 4.30pm. At 5pm, outside a large glass of wine, I remembered Annette. Oops. Hoping it wasn't too late I sent her a message saying I was out for the next hour so, if she had the results, could she please leave them in the post box and I would sort payment with Cara. I felt guilty about this, but I needn't have because when we got back there was nothing in the post box.

I checked the post box again at 6.15pm. Nothing. I checked again at 6.30pm. Still nothing. At 7pm I cracked and sent a text to Cara asking if I should be worried. It was a dumb question because regardless of whether I should be worried or not, I already was.

Cara replied saying she would call Annette and within minutes sent me a second message saying 'print this'. It was a photo of the blood results. Before I got to the printer, I received another text, this time from Annette with the same photo, then a voice message from her telling me to print the photo. We made the deadline, I had what I needed, and it was 7.30pm. Phew.

Then there was a knock at the door. I opened it to the freezing cold, pitch black night and found Annette on my doorstep holding "a fresh copy" of the results for me. "Just in case you feel better having the actual results".

Covid notwithstanding, I almost hugged her. Not for the first time I thought how lucky I was to be going through this here in Italy. Specifically, in this tiny little community halfway up a mountain in the middle of Italy. I know everyone wants to be at 'home' in a crisis and especially with the NHS but at that precise moment I could not had been gladder to be here.

5 BRING OUT THE BIG SCARY MACHINES

The first Big Scary Machine, a holding hand, a friendly face, a crying baby and a reckoning up. Oh, and a Covid benefit.

February 3rd

I remember this as the day they first brought out the Big Scary Machines (capital letters intended). The alarm went off at 5.30am and we dragged ourselves out of bed at a quarter to 6. Himself had remembered to change the time on the heating but even so, as we showered and dressed, it felt brutal.

When we left the house (an hour later) dawn was breaking and the mountains looked amazing. The light was so fabulous that I briefly - very briefly – thought it was worth getting up so early just to see it. That was of course, utter nonsense. Nothing is ever worth getting up that early, except for maybe a flight to somewhere hot and exotic.

After picking Cara up at her house we drove to the scan centre in Chieti arriving exactly on time. The centre was near the hospital but not directly a part of it so I was glad we had Cara with us, She trained in Chieti so knew exactly where we should be going.

At reception there were more forms to sign and they initially said Cara could not go in with me but then added (talking about me) "unless she needs help with translation". Cara and I grinned at each other. Success! She promptly declared that I couldn't cope without translation while I tried to look blank. I confess it was pretty easy as I'd had a lot of recent practice at looking confused.

I was especially pleased that Cara had snuck under the radar when we got to the admission office and discovered yet another set of forms to be completed and a heap of questions to be answered. Most of the questions were straightforward – repeats of the previous ones - but some were quite technical and Cara was invaluable for clarification. To my chagrin they only glanced at the blood test results that I had agonised over before adding them to the pile of forms.

After this, Cara had to leave – the special dispensation only went as far as the admission interview and I was sent into the corridor to wait until I was called through for the scan. It wasn't long.

The scan technician (Doctor) arrived to collect me and apprehensively asked if I could understand any Italian. Obviously, word had spread. But he asked me in Italian which I thought was quite funny.

I reassured him that I understood 'enough' and he

visibly relaxed. He showed me the changing room, handed me a gown and told me to take all my top clothing off (leave the bottom half) and then tie the gown with the opening at the front. As I was changing he knocked on the door frame and checked I'd remembered to not wear anything with metal, and if I hadn't then I should take anything metal off now. I felt insulted – as if Id do something as stupid as wear something metal.

Coming out again, I was handed over to a nurse. She immediately took my lovely 'fresh out of the packet' face mask away and gave me a different one. Ok, I admit I might have forgotten that my face mask was the type with a metal bar in it. I liked the new one better. It was the type that ties around your head, so I looked like a glamorous surgeon in ER.[7]

She put a tourniquet on my arm, slid a long needle into a vein at my wrist, then injected fluid into it. The needle was enormous. I mean so EEEEEnormous that I screwed my eyes shut and turned my head so as not to see it happening. The nurse exclaimed aloud and stopped, thinking she'd hurt me and I turned back to say it was okay, I just didn't want to see it happening. All of which caused me to see the needle going in anyway. Bummer.

The nurse passed me back to the technician who wasn't quite ready so I stood in the doorway and watched him preparing for me. That was probably a mistake. I really didn't like the look of all those bottles of fluid which I (correctly) thought might be about to be connected to the tube hanging out of my wrist. So instead, I studied the Big Scary Machine that took up most of the room. If you've never seen an MRI

---

[7] Yeah I know. In my dreams.

machine it is basically a huge tube with a bed type thing sticking out of it that inserts you into the tube. For all its size, the space inside the tube itself looked quite cosy. Claustrophobic is the word I'm looking for. Not for the last time I wondered who invents these things.

The technician finished with his bottles, called me in, and ran the same battery of questions at me that I'd now answered three times. Did I have any metal inside my body? was I allergic? Had I ever had a contrast before. No, no and no.

Satisfied, he told me to lay face down on the bed, indicating where my head went and where I should lay so my breasts would be positioned above two holes. I went to take the gown off and he threw his hands up "No, no. You keep that on, keep that on".

Like me, you might have assumed he meant for modesty's sake. Like me, you would have been wrong. As soon as I was in position with my titties hanging down through the holes he took hold of them, one by one, and manhandled them into the right position. Hardly modest. Then he repositioned my legs and moved my arms inwards. With my head down I couldn't see anything, but I was aware of the bed moving into the tube. It stopped, and he moved my arms again, further inwards. I was right. There's not a lot of space in those things.

Lastly, he placed a huge pair of earphones over my head and pressed something into my hand. I couldn't see what it was. He positioned my thumb over it and told me it was an alarm bell. "If you feel panic, you must press it" he said. 'Hang on' I wanted to say, 'what is there to panic about? What aren't you telling me?' But it was too late, I could hear the door to the room closing already.

Then it began.

It was incredibly, unbelievably noisy.

Clank, bang, clank. But more like CLANK BANG CLANK, over and over again.

I tried to distract myself. First I thought of a person I know who creates music from everyday sounds. She'd love this I thought. Then I tried to visualise calm and peaceful places I had been to. None of it worked because the noise was so loud and so random. It was impossible to adjust to, because it changed all the time. Then boom!

I heard a sudden, very loud voice in my earphones.

"The contrast arrives! Do not be afraid."

Coming out of the blue like that, it was terrifying. If I'd had enough room to jump out of my skin I probably would have. As it was, by the time I'd recovered from the shock of the voice and translated what it said, the noise level had increased exponentially, and I could already feel something cold and deadly making its way up inside my arm. Yuck.

More noise. And more. I lost all track of time. When it finally stopped my ears rang with silence. There was movement but by now I was so disorientated I couldn't tell if I was moving forward or backwards. My ears adjusted and I heard the door opening.

I sensed rather than heard footsteps and the earphones

were taken off. He smiled at me. "It's finished". he said.

He sat me up and told me to sit for a moment. When he was happy I wouldn't keel over he directed me back to the nurse station where I found a different (male) nurse waiting to take the needle out of my vein. Holding a pad against the tiny wound ("only very lightly you understand") I went to get dressed and then, as instructed, walked along another corridor to my third waiting room of the day.

En-route I met a woman who seemed to know me. Her face lit up. "How are you?" she asked. "Have you just had your scan? Was everything okay?" If we weren't living under Covid and both wearing masks I just knew she would have hugged and double kissed me by now but I didn't know who she was.

Then I realised.

It was the doctor who had done my biopsy and who told me I had cancer. I knew her in a lab coat with her hair tied up. Now she was wearing outdoor clothes with her long hair floating over her shoulders. I felt bad that I hadn't recognised her and somehow very grateful that she'd recognised me. After my first encounter with a Big Scary Machine it was nice to realise that people saw me as a person, not just a process. It was something I came to appreciate more and more as my journey went on.

-0-

In the waiting room there was a woman with a tiny baby, who was taken away for a procedure while I was there. She looked so scared and helpless as she watched her baby being taken away. I'm convinced it's sometimes harder for parents/partners/carers (delete as appropriate) than it is for the patient. Just sitting and waiting, unable to help and with nothing to focus on has to be a torture. I was trying to formulate a sentence to say to the baby's mother when the doctor (my biopsy doctor as I now thought of her – I was amassing a collection of my doctors) came back and told me I could go, so the words never got said.

-0-

Outside the building again, I heard my name being called. It was Cara, inside in the reception area. She waved at me and I waited. I hadn't seen her there. I hadn't to be honest, even looked, thinking she would have left and had a coffee with Himself or something.

She told me she had come back inside to wait for me. Did I have the results? I said no so we both went back inside and she asked the people at reception when I could have them. I know for a fact that if I had asked I would have been waved away, but this being Cara they went off to see if we could have them straight away. While we were waiting, I told Cara about the third waiting room and how I just sat there, then was told I could go. She said they would have been checking my MRI for lumps over and above the existing one and, had they found anything new, they would had done another biopsy there and then. Ergo, being told I could leave was good news. I liked that. I liked hearing good news

The man from reception came back and said no I had to come back in a week for the full report, so we left, stopping in Guardiagrele for coffee at Boys with Beards before going home.

February 4th

I remember reading somewhere (I think it was Linus in a peanuts cartoon) that 'no problem is too big or scary to run away from'. I'd always thought that was a good philosophy but to be honest, it wasn't not really working for me anymore.

I made a determined effort to face up to what was happening and narrowed it down to five scenarios, from best to worst case. They were

I'd have to have a lumpectomy

I'd have to have a lumpectomy followed by radiotherapy

I'd have to have a lumpectomy followed by chemotherapy

I'd have to have a mastectomy and radiotherapy

I'd have to have a mastectomy with chemotherapy[8]

I didn't include the worst possible scenario (dying) because that was too scary. Anyway, now I knew it hasn't spread to the lymph nodes it was no longer on the table. I was one of the lucky ones.

I deliberately didn't think about the whole breast reconstruction issue because it was out of my control. Instead, I focused on chemotherapy which I dreaded, and on two things in particular; the sickness and the hair loss.

-0-

---

[8] Later on I learned that some people had both radiotherapy and chemotherapy. I'm glad I didn't know that at the time.

At this point I was about 10 days past when I should have had my hair cut and I looked like a neglected sheepdog with greying roots. To say it was an untidy mess would be an understatement but, knowing I might have to have chemotherapy and lose it all, it seemed a waste to get it cut and coloured. I'd rather put the money towards a decent wig.

I dyed it myself instead. It sort of worked: the colour looked okay but the condition was something approaching scorched hay and it was still a straggly mess. Nonetheless I was a lot happier than I was. If chemotherapy wasn't needed I could be at the hairdressers immediately, and if it was, I'd just put 70 euros towards my wig collection. Looking back this shows me just how depressed I was. All my frugality did was to make me even more miserable every time I looked in the mirror. I'd never make that mistake again. I'd do everything I could to keep my morale a bit higher.

The other mistake I made was browsing for wigs on the internet. it was months before I stopped seeing wig advertisements on my social media feeds. In the end I had to start browsing for bizarre items (foam paving slabs, solar powered sunbeds, weed seeds) to scramble the algorithm. Even so, it forever.

February 5th

Immediately after my scan I had these weird red marks on my skin. They vanished to be replaced by another memento - a small lump mid-way between my breasts and about an inch below. It was exactly where the top of the weird red marks had been and it was very itchy and irritating.

In other news Cristina was back from Rome where her operation had been postponed even as she was checking in for it. Her test for COVID-19 was positive and, as she had barely left the house since her first operation way before Christmas, she was (rightly) furious. I sympathised. The thought of being psyched up for an operation for months, finally getting to within hours of having it and then being told no, go home again was too awful to contemplate.

February 6th

The commune had organised a COVID-19 screening (free, voluntary) for all citizens so we booked an appointment for 5.36pm. Yes, it was an odd time but everyone was staggered at 12 minutes intervals for safety. Outside the tiny local school they were using as the test centre, Civil Defence Volunteers checked people in and out to keep us separate. Covered head to foot with hazard suits and masks they looked like the scientists in ET[9]. Then they pulled out the ubiquitous pile of multiple forms to sign and everything felt reassuringly normal again.

The test itself – delivered by Cara - was not great. The one I had had before was uncomfortable but now they'd changed the technique. Instead of the nose and throat they just swabbed inside the nostrils – but so far inside that the swab felt like it might be poking the back of your eyeballs at any second. It was eye watering and not in a good way.

February 7th

The COVID-19 results came through at 8am and I was

---

[9] The bit where they kidnapped ET from the house.

negative. At 8.04am Cristina contacted me to say she and her family had also tested negative. If she was furious about her cancelled operation before, she was now positively stratospheric with anger. At 8pm the commune published the results from the whole community – 45% of the population went for testing and it was 100% negative.

February 9th

I went to Vasto shopping with two friends. Unfortunately, most of Vasto was closed.

Cristina told me she was going back to Rome tomorrow, ready for her rescheduled operation. I kind of envied her.

February 10th

Having cancer got me bumped up the priority list for the Covid vaccine (to first dibs with the over 80s) so I went to the commune to sign up. It was remarkably simple and I was a bit shocked by that. My details were written onto multiple forms, I signed everything – a mere 5 signatures this time and "e fatto!" - I should expect a phone call telling me where and when to go. It was no more than 5 minutes from start to finish.

Sign up done, I drove home to pick Himself up and then to Chieti (together) to pick the scan results up. I signed a receipt for them at the reception desk and scurried back to the car, anxious to see what they had said. The CD I obviously couldn't look at, but I scanned the written report with Google Translate and it confirmed that no cancer had been detected in my lymph nodes. I was thrilled. Now I was adjusting to the idea that I had cancer I could celebrate the small mercies. I sent a copy to Cara while Himself was still driving home.

11th February

Up until the MRI scan, waiting for the biopsy after the mammogram, and then waiting for the biopsy results had been the worst part.

Once I had the confirmation of cancer there was actually a sense of relief because I'd already convinced myself it was cancer anyway, and having a result meant we could get on and do something about it. On this basis, the MRI scan should have felt like progress but it actually felt like a delay. In my head I knew it was necessary and part of the process, but in my heart I felt like I was having to wait passively again, and I hated it. I wanted to be at the 'this is what do we do about it' stage. Having a plan, whatever that plan is, was my first step to getting rid of this and I just wanted it to happen NOW.

Anyway, I had to be patient. Cara was finding out what my next steps should be ...

-0-

In the afternoon I had a text from Cristina. She had been admitted to a ward and her operation would be tomorrow. I wondered what you did with yourself, trapped in a hospital bed the night before an operation you were dreading, when you actually felt perfectly well. I decided it must be awful, being all alone in a hospital without being too sedated to care, and I hoped I wouldn't have to do that. I made a mental note to ask her when she came out. I forget my mental note, so I still don't know.

12th February

Cara called me early in the morning to say Ortona hospital would call me next week to give me an appointment. An hour later I was in the shoe repair shop picking up my favourite blue boots when Ortona hospital called me "Be there tomorrow at 10.30" they said. Gulp.

6 MEET ONCOLOGY

Peril in the snow, a decision, a dud Valentine's Day, an even dudder chocolate cake and two new bras.

February 13th

When we woke up it had snowed and the still-dark sky was heavy with more to come. Given the depth of snow already on the ground we left earlier than planned and it was well that we did. The carabinieri were out in force, checking peoples' permission to be on the roads and we crossed fingers that we wouldn't be stopped and delayed. Snow ploughs were also out, but the snow was filling up the roads as fast as they were cleared. Driving was slow and painful.

Approaching Guardiagrele the car skidded on ice and we veered off towards the inadequate barrier that was supposed to stop us sliding down the mountain. My stomach lurched in fear but Himself managed to control the car and pulled it back to the centre of the road where it slewed again to head directly towards a car on the other side. I was too shocked and scared even to scream. I genuinely thought we were about to collide head on and, from the expression on the other driver's face, he thought the same thing. We missed each other by centimetres and I remember thinking how ironic it would have been to die on my way to an appointment that was all about saving my life.

We had already been driving slower than a snail with a limp but now, off the main roads, we drove even slower, almost doubling the normal journey time. For once, leaving so early had paid off. We weren't actually late.

This time, knowing exactly where to go, I went confidently to the room the nurses were in. I'll be honest, I felt a bit smug about that. It didn't last long. I was immediately reminded of how out of my depth I was when a nurse shouted at me for not staying behind the yellow (Covid) line. I didn't even know there was a yellow line.

-0-

I got my ticket (number 27) and waited. Before long (in fact I think it may actually have been right on time) I was called into an examination room and once again stripped off. This was for another ultrasound of my breast.

Afterward, with the goo wiped off and fully dressed again I sat down in front of a desk. Opposite sat a doctor and, next to him, a nurse. They asked for my scan results and I handed over the CD of the scan. While the doctor was looking at it on the computer he asked me what size my breasts were. I said I didn't know what they were in Italian sizing, but in English I was trent'quattro effa. "What?" they asked. "What? Were they 3? Were they 4?" I assumed they were referring to the cup size but it made no difference, because I simply didn't know. I said so and they looked at each other and shrugged in a way that definitely expressed disdain for the type of woman who didn't even know her own bra size[10].

Then we got down to it. I was told "the lymph nodes are ok so we can leave those although maybe remove some just to be on the safe side. The lump though has to come out". 'Well that's fairly direct' I thought.

The doctor explained that they would do a lumpectomy "but you should understand that this is not a small lump and it is very deep so we may (on the operating table) decide that the whole breast should be removed. In which case there will be a reconstruction".

Oh shit. I tried to sound calm but I'd be lying if I didn't admit that my voice quavered.

"Um, could you tell me when the reconstruction might be?".

They both looked slightly shocked at my question, and he frowned at me. I knew, I just knew how vain and ridiculous I sounded. I knew they were thinking how pathetic I was. Except I was wrong. He proved it when said, sounding slightly bewildered, "It will be at the same time of course".

Of course, it was of course. I was in Italy. The idea of a woman without breasts was just ridiculous - naturally they would do it at the same time. By now I was mentally skipping up the walls and grinning like an idiot under my mask.

---

[10] I thought of looking for the European size on the label of the bra I was wearing but it was so old and the label so faded it was impossible to read. In fairness, it was a favourite bra.

They gave me a fresh set of forms to sign, mainly saying that I'd understood everything. I looked but there wasn't anything more accurate like 'I think and hope I've understood everything but I really can't swear to it' I could sign instead, so I crossed my fingers and signed the lie. Then I signed consent forms for the next stages and I was told the pre-op checks would be the next Tuesday. Ooh, that was unexpectedly soon!

Did I have any other questions they wanted to know. Well, only about a hundred. I asked how long I would be waiting for the operation and he said probably between 20-30 days. I checked my notes on all the other questions I wanted to ask even though I knew them by heart and decided all I really needed to ask was the biggie … what other treatment might I need after the operation?

I was thinking about chemotherapy of course, and I'd braced myself for bad news. He couldn't tell me. All that would be decided depending on the operation. I was even more certain now that this would be a mastectomy and thought 'well, if it is a mastectomy with immediate reconstruction and it saves me going through chemotherapy, I would be happy with that. Happy was the wrong word. it was the better option of all the bad options was really what I was thinking.

When I came out it felt as if I'd just lived through a lifetime and I was bemused that it was still morning. Not even lunchtime. The snow was still falling and the roads were still icy. We drove the longer route home via the main roads and I was glad we did. We passed a head on collision on the way and I shivered, remembering how nearly that had been us.

At home, I sent Cara the information. Snow notwithstanding, she said she'd come over the next day - to see me and talk it through. I offered to make tea and chocolate cake. It was the very least I could think of.

February 14th

It was Valentine's Day and we had a table booked forklunch. It would have been dinner but Covid restrictions had closed restaurants in the evening. Except now we didn't even have the lunch option because the government had just clamped down again and closed all the restaurants and bars. Completely. We were going nowhere. It was the worst Valentine's Day in the history of Valentines Days

I texted Cristina to see how she was. Her operation is done and dusted so, weather and road conditions permitting, she was coming home today. I envied her.

It was a depressing day – still snowy and very cold – so I huddled in the kitchen to make the chocolate cake for Cara's visit. It took forever, used a ton of ingredients and was one of the worst cakes I've ever made. The fudgy chocolate icing was way too sweet, and the cake was way too dry. It looked delicious but that only made it worse. To Cara's credit she managed to eat half a slice, which was more than I could do. As soon as she left I threw the whole thing away.

Over tea and cake (how English were we being?) Cara gave me the low down on being an inpatient in an Italian hospital. I've only ever been an inpatient in the UK for one night so my hospital knowledge was almost zero and I needed all the information I could absorb. The most surprising thing she told me was that I needed to take a small tablecloth type thing with me for my meals. I was so obviously bewildered by this dainty concept that she insisted she would lend me one. I needed cutlery too apparently, although she said the food was so rubbish I was unlikely to eat very much.

We also discussed bra sizes. When I repeated what I told the doctor (trent'quattro effa) she looked equally bewildered and it was apparent that merely translating my English size isn't enough. I checked English vs European clothing sizes on my phone but when I finally announced what thought the right size was, she refused to believe me so I had to take my habitually oversized jumper off to display the full horror of overly-generous breasts. Even so, she asked to see a bra so she could measure it – she'd never heard of an Italian G cup size. I should mention that Cara is was blessed with the type of blissfully small and neat breasts I haven't had since I was about 18.

Eventually we agreed I should go and buy a new bra here in Italy and get myself measured. I wasn't sure why knowing my bra size was so important; except I supposed if they were making me a new breast it really needed to match the one they were leaving behind on the other side. Or maybe, I thought, they gave you some special bra to wear while you were healing.

We put my bras away and agreed that knowing things like bra sizes was far more important in learning a language than conjugations. After Cara left, I looked up the word for bra. It was reggiseno. Now I knew by now that seno was breast and I figured the first part was a verb so I looked up reggiere and it said to hold up. That's brilliant. The literal translation for bra is 'to hold up breast'. Or breast holder-upper if you prefer. This was definitely my word of the day.

15th February

In the morning I re-read all my notes and my cancer dictionary. Because I had an Italian lesson booked, I was tempted to ask if we could practise but as I hadn't told my teacher it wasn't really an option. Besides, I knew I knew what I needed to know. (still with me?). I checked on my lump which was now very easily felt. It seemed to me to be getting larger daily but I know that wasn't the case because all three of my ultrasound reports measured it as the same size.

After my lesson I went to the lingerie shop. It was, as Cara had promised, open for customers even though we were back in a Covid red zone. You have to love a country that classifies book shops and bra shops as life essentials.

Here it's not possible to say 'just looking thanks' when you go into a shop. You are either ignored completely while the sales assistant talks to someone on the telephone, or you are helped whether you like it or not. This was one of the helped whether you like it or not occasions. I had thought I'd nip in, get measured and pick up a single bra. No. I was shown into a small changing room (mercifully with a portable heater inside) and given a selection of 6 bras in the size I thought I wanted.

I tried one on and she came to look. She looked at me and wrinkled her nose. "Wait here".

Another 6 bras arrived, in sizes either side of the size I wanted because, as she told me, different brands vary in size.

No kidding Sherlock. Then, once we kind of agreed on what size I needed I also had to try on different designs. By the end, knee deep in lace and wires, I think I must have tried on well over 20 bras, and I'd been in there so long that I felt way too guilty to just buy the one I'd intended. Which was a bummer because they were horrendously expensive.

I chose two. They were a good choice. I know this because she told me so. She said the minimiser bra I bought was perfect for "being comfortable." and the second one was perfect for going out when (and I quote) "you are entering the room with your breasts proudly in front of you".

From the changes in her tone when she talked about the two bras it was clear to me that the first, comfortable, bra was not supposed to be worn very often. Probably only on fat days when you were hiding indoors.

7 A TALE OF TWO SURGEONS

Blood mucus bones and breathing. Falling in love with a smiley surgeon, meeting the morgue and snubbing the plastic surgeon.

February 16th

We dragged ourselves out of bed at 5.30 am. By the time we left at 6.30 the scenery was so beautiful I almost understood people who enjoy getting up at dawn. It was a postcard fantasy. The warm orange lights of the small hamlets flickered against the dark of the slopes of the mountains; the snowy peaks were dramatically edged against the indigo sky; and a red glow of dawn was just beginning to be visible. That's enough over-blown imagery. More pragmatically, the roads were clear.

We arrived at the hospital at 7.35am and I went straight to the waiting room where there were already about 8 people waiting. We all sat and waited for 8am, watching the doctors and nurses arrive for work. People braver than I wandered down corridors to ask questions and were all chased back. I was glad I want the only one clearly confused about what was supposed to be happening.

When my name was finally announced I think I was about the 5th to be called. I sat down with a nurse who sternly directed me to disinfect my hands (my third time since arriving) before giving me yet more forms to sign. When I had signed everything she explained the process for the day, speaking so fast I was instantly worried I'd forget everything before she'd even finished. I grabbed a pen from her desk (earning myself a frown) and started scribbling the key instructions on the outside of my note file. It was sensible but pointless because later, when I tried to consult it, my panicked scribble was actually illegible. The bit I did understand immediately was where she said I should go for breakfast after the first two procedures.

Her assistant (hereon in called nurse 2) took over at this point and took 5 phials of my blood before giving me a COVID-19 test. This time I was prepared for the swab to feel like it was poking into my brain. Being prepared didn't help though.

Drained of blood and mucus, I went back to the waiting room to wait for an ECG. I sat and sat. Then the person who went in to see nurse 1 and nurse 2 right after me arrived and took a supermarket ticket from a little machine on the wall. Damn. I hadn't realised I was meant to take a ticket. I got one. It was number 16 and, as the number showing on the board was 7, I thought I might as well read the book I brought with me. Affecting an unconvincing air of casualness I opened my kindle and began to read; stopping every few minutes to check the display board. I don't know why I did this because there were aural announcements too, plus nurses to escort the patients in each time. There was no chance of missing my slot, but I couldn't relax.

A particular fiery nurse emerged from nowhere to survey the people in the room. It was obvious to her, as it was to me, that several people had disobeyed the COVID rules to bring partners or relatives with them. Hands on hips she bellowed that anyone who was not with a person who couldn't walk unaided could leave right now.

"Haven't you heard of COVID?" she yelled. "What is wrong with you all? That is IT. Get out now. Yes, I mean you as well!" she swung round and wagged a finger at the people behind her. Roughly a third of the people in the room sheepishly got up and filed out. "And don't come back!" she shouted after them. "I'll be checking".

The display got to 14 and I put the book away. It turned to the number 15 but the woman who was after me and now before me wasn't paying attention and she almost missed it. In fact, she only realised just at the second it clicked to number 16 and dashed inside. I couldn't follow. It was strictly one at a time, so this meant that my number had been and gone without me. I got out of my seat and stood jiggling from foot to foot; ready to dive in as soon as the next technician was available.

The display clicked and the announcement called for number 17. A sweet old man, clutching a 17 ticket in his shaking hand, got up and headed for the entrance but I got

[11] I checked when I came out and he wasn't there so he must have gone in straight after me.

75

their first and physically blocked his way. Gesticulating for him to get back, I explained to the nurse/escort that they hadn't actually done number 16 yet and that was me. He was actually a very sweet old man and I did feel quite mean[11] but if I hadn't done it, then I'd still be there now.

-0-

The ECG was simple and not invasive. Basically, you just stripped off and lay still while electrodes were attached to you. The two young guys who did it were quite chatty and fascinated by my Englishness. 'What did I do? Where did I come from? What was I doing here?'. One of them was a poet in his spare time and he was telling me about his work, but I got more than a bit lost in the detail. It was nice to chat though. They did the test twice before they were satisfied and told me I could go.

I consulted my notes (I hadn't reached the illegible bits yet) and headed to the basement to find the bar for breakfast. Breakfast was a cornetto (croissant) and cappuccino. I was ravenous by now but the relief of taking my mask off for a few minutes was actually the best part.

-0-

After breakfast I replaced my mask and went to floor one to find the x-ray department. When I couldn't find it, I stopped and asked at a desk. It turned out that this desk was the reception for X-ray, just without any signs or notices to indicate what it might be. She gave me a number (number 10 this time) and told me to go through the door on the right to the waiting room.

I wasn't there long before I was called. That was fortuitous because this room was a particularly bilious shade of pink. The slight orange tinge to it made it even more objectionable than the other pink waiting room, which had more of a fuchsia hue. I was glad to get out of it.

Buoyed by my experience with the lovely chatty ECG boys I beamed at the woman doing my x-ray. She gave me the death stare back. To say she was slightly brusque was an understatement. Far from being interesting to her, my Englishness was not interesting was just a pain in the neck and she wasn't inclined to explain anything. To be fair I could understand why, and the process was so straightforward (take your top clothes off, stand here, put your arms here) that it didn't matter.

-0-

Out of X-ray I consulted my notes again and eventually deciphered that I should be back on Floor 3, and that I should go back to the office where I'd had the blood tests. So I did. Except when I got to the corridor I couldn't remember which of the identical doors the office was. I'd have to casually loiter and ask someone.

Trying not to look too loitery, I studied the portraits of women that were lining the corridor. It was the first time I had noticed them although I'd by now been up and down this corridor several times. Each one was a cancer survivor and there was a small biography attached, They were technically very good and the stories uplifting; they really should have been bigger and in the main reception area.

I was wondering who I could tell this to when I spotted

nurse 2 in the process of escorting someone else somewhere else. I waved in my casual loitery 'oh hi I'm not really lost' sort of way but she saw straight through me and told me to wait where I was. She would come and get me. After just a few minutes more she did but, instead of taking me into the blood test room I was expecting, we went into a consulting room opposite.

-0-

The white-coated woman sitting behind the desk was small, with a mass of dark curly hair and very smiley. She was so smiley I instantly wanted her to be my friend. It turned out that she would be my surgeon, which was almost better. She told me she would be doing my lumpectomy. Or maybe mastectomy, she added.

She had a positive mountain of forms for me to sign, most significantly all the consent forms. There is something very daunting about signing consent forms, even in your own language. I've now discovered that signing consent forms in another language without reading them (nobody has that kind of time to spare) is even more daunting. There was no point in thinking about it. They had to be signed if I wanted an operation, and I did. I think I scribbled my signature on 7 forms in total, plus answering all the questions I had already answered the other day and more besides.

We took a break halfway through the forms so I could take my clothes off and have my breast photographed. It wasn't exactly page three, but it meant another consent form to sign for photo release.

I concentrated very hard as she ran through the

procedures and initially managed to follow her, but the longer it went on the more worried I became that I was missing things. So I asked if I could record it. "No" she said, but only because she was about to give me a sheet with everything written on. She pushed it across the table and I read it as quickly as I could.

"Do you understand it?"

"Yes"

"Can you confirm you have understood?"

"Yes", I confirmed, "I've understood everything".

"In that case", she continued, "the most important thing you need to know right now is that you must go to Chieti hospital the day before the operation for another lymph nodes exam".

I thought I'd already done whole lymph nodes thing with the biopsy but maybe they are like COVID-19 tests – only really good for the day you have them. She told me that they wouldn't be telling me the results this time, but they'd give me an envelope with the photos and I had to bring this with me when I arrived for the operation. This was apparently so they could decide what to do about the lymph nodes on the day.

She reiterated that she would be removing the lump and there was a lot of talk about the area being clean and needing to make sure the lymph were okay and the size of the lump and so on. This was her preamble to announcing that, if necessary, they would do a mastectomy. So I would also need to talk with the plastic surgeon.

While I'm still nodding one of the nurses (call her nurse 3 on that day - they kept coming in and out) said the plastic surgeon isn't in today. My smiley surgeon said she thought he was. So they had a discussion about if he was in or not. At least I think that's what they were saying — it was a matter of me grabbing every fourth word and filling in the gaps. Eventually they concluded (again I think) that he was and that I should see him(her?) but that I may need to wait awhile. Nurse 2 would take me.

I was given some more forms to complete — one for when I come back for the operation and another to do now, while I was waiting. I was also given a prescription which I had to get from the pharmacy downstairs. I wasn't sure but I thought this was for something I had to do the night before the operation. It had seemed a little weird to me but given the list of things I needed to do the day before maybe it wasn't. I asked when the operation would be, and she said she didn't know exactly but it would be between 20 and 30 days.

The junior nurse took me back to the main waiting room and told me to wait. She got me a number (number 14) and said that when it was called I should go into the first office on the right. I waited for maybe half an hour before I was called. It was not, as I was expecting, the plastic surgeon but the anaesthetist and I decided that I must had misunderstood the earlier conversation about seeing the plastic surgeon. The stress of never quite being positive I had understood what I'd been told was getting to me.

-0-

The anaesthetist asked for the forms I had just filled in, then asked me more questions. Nurse 4 took my blood pressure while I was doing this and then I had even more forms to sign. My blood tests arrived from earlier and while the anaesthetist studied them I mused on the disconcerting crucifix on the wall. Disconcerting to me that is, I'm sure they are reassuring to other people.

The anaesthetist interrupted my musing to say my cholesterol was exceptionally high, which shocked me so much I swear my blood pressure rose up to join it. What I wanted to ask is 'will this affect the operation' but while I was still composing the question she answered it for me. "You'll need to sort that out after the operation" she told me.

Finally, she told me that on the day of the operation I should expect to have both a local and general anaesthetic and that was it. I asked her if I was now done for the day, and she said yes.

-0-

When I left her office, still worrying about not understanding if I had to see a plastic surgeon or not, I thought maybe I should double check that I really was done. I looked for nurse 2 but she was nowhere in sight, so I waited about 5 minutes, hoping to see a face (any face) I recognised. Nobody appeared and, as I didn't want to knock on any of the doors and intrude, I hovered for a few more minutes then went to find the pharmacy.

The pharmacy was in the basement and, like everything, not very well signposted. I did several circuits of the wide empty corridors until I found it. It was near the morgue. I mention this because I've never been that close to a morgue before. I've never been anywhere near a morgue in fact. I don't suppose many of us have. Anyway, the prescription turned out to be for a packet of 10 prefilled syringes. The pharmacist told me I should use the first one the night before the operation and then use one a day when I came home again. I'd forgotten that it was normal here to do injections yourself and I gulped. This was going to be a challenge.

-0-

Back outside I got into the car with Himself and read my instructions again. It seemed I had to source a plain white cotton bra with no wires to wear post-op. If I'd known that before I went to the bra shop, I might have made different choices. This bra business was getting expensive[12].

We were maybe a third of the way home when my phone rang. It was the hospital. Roughly translated, they wanted to know where the hell I was because they were searching all over for me and the plastic surgeon was waiting. Shit.

I said I hadn't realised, that I had left but I would come back immediately. I said it would take me fifteen minutes to get there. In truth it would be more like twenty-five minutes but fifteen didn't sound as bad. I could hear excited conversation at the other end then the voice came back to me.

"It's too late now. You will have to come back on Friday morning instead and be here at 8.30".

I meekly agreed, mortified at how dumb I had been. I told Himself that I'd drive myself this time as there was no

---

[12] I had no idea just how expensive it would get.

point in us both getting up ridiculously early, but he said no, he wanted to come.

My word of the day was incosciente, which means unconscious. It was on the defibrillator instructions.

It's worth mentioning that I saw 10 professionals that day. That's not including tangential nurses and various support roles like pharmacy and admin. If all the people who had helped me so far were on my Christmas list, I would have been bankrupt by January.

February 19th

Three days later I was up at 6.30am and ready to leave at 7.15. An appalling night's sleep had left me exhausted so I was glad that Himself had overruled me on the driving issue. He told me he had figured that, as its only one person I was seeing this time, he wouldn't have to hang around waiting too long. He was so wrong.

I was skulking outside the secretariat hoping to check in 10 minutes early when my smiley surgeon from Tuesday came by. She recognised me (I told you she was nice) and knew why I was there. "Just wait in the main waiting room" she said, "and you'll be seen later".

8.30 came and went. When it got to 9.30 I sent a text Himself to tell him I thought I might be a while yet. To be fair, he'd probably already worked that out, and replied saying he'd go for a drive and see if he could get a coffee somewhere. I started reading my book but none of it was really sinking in. Even now I have no idea what book it was a I read during all these appointments. 45 minutes later (10.15) a nurse came into the waiting room and asked if anyone was there for Dottore Roberto. I took the usual pause to translate and a slightly longer pause to realise that I recognised the name and jumped to my feet to shout me, that's me just as she was turning to leave. And I did shout. There is no room for British reticence when you are about to miss your meeting for the second time.

While I had been in the waiting room I had seen a man wandering in out, noticeable for his height. bald pate, and cadaverous looking appearance. This turned out to be Dottore Roberto. He was not what I was expecting, but then I was not who he was expecting. My name was not even on his list. He seemed annoyed (with the nurse, not me) and I intervened to explain that it was my fault because I was supposed to be there on Tuesday but that seemed to make him even more impatient.

He held a hand up. "Just tell me your name". I did. He gave me that look of incomprehension that normally follows hearing my name and I repeated it. He shook his head. "Write it down". I handed it to him on a scrap of paper and he searched for me on the computer, found me and despatched the nurse to find my file. She was back with it almost immediately and he began reading though it. He was silent. The room was silent. I was silent. I just sat there looking at my file as he turned the pages and thinking how incredibly fat it was considering I wasn't even on the health system's radar a few months ago.

He closed the file and asks me about existing medical conditions. This was about the 6th time I'd answered this question and the answer was still none. Except this time, in an effort to lighten the atmosphere I jokingly added "except cancer of course". Either the joke didn't work in Italian or it was just not funny because he didn't smile. I suspect both.

Did I mention I was shivering? Knowing that I'd probably be having to strip off every 5 seconds, I'd put just a thin jumper on that morning. Which was fine in the over-heated waiting room but he had the windows open in his consulting room. They were only open a crack but it was February.

A few seconds later I didn't even have my jumper because I'd stripped it off to lay down on the couch. On my back with my arms over my head I watched him as he examined my breasts. His examination was subtly more determined than anyone else so far but I couldn't put my finger on why. Less diagnostic and more investigative, I think.

He asked me for my mammogram, and I said it was in my file on his desk (which I thought it was – I was fairly certain they took it off me last time). The nurse looked, found a disc and loaded it into the computer. He left me to look at it and it was the wrong disc – it was the disc from the scan. I felt for her. She tried again and this time he studied it for what seemed ages, then came back and had another feel. Finally, he told me to sit up and dangle my legs over the side.

He pulled up a chair to sit directly in front and below of me and pulled a pen from his pocket. First, he drew on me, making notes as he went. Then he started measuring and writing numbers on me too. The nurse came over and copied the numbers onto a piece of paper. Finally, he looked at me asked me what I knew about what I had. I said a bit. He began to tell me about my lump, and I told him my understanding that it was both deep and large, and that a mastectomy or least a partial mastectomy might be needed. He confirmed that it would be – so now it was definite.

He talked some more about my lymph nodes and what might or might not happen depending on the results of the Chieti tests just before the operation, also on what they find when I am on the table. Finally, he asked me my bra size (Hurrah! this time I could answer) and pulled a book from his pocket. I could see it was a catalogue of silicone implants. Who knew you could get titties by mail order? He found the right page (based on my size I guess) then, looking at the numbers he had written on me, gave the nurse a set of reference numbers. He told me that the intention was to reconstruct my breast so it was as nearly as possible the same as the remaining one.

That was it. I took wipes and some cleanser from the nurse and looked into the mirror to clean myself up. I couldn't believe how much scribble there was over me and almost didn't want to clean it off so I could show it to himself. It was like a bizarre work of art. Then I noticed the nurse looking at me with a 'what's taking her so long' expression and thought better of it. I sloshed the goo and began wiping.

With my thin jumper pulled back over my slightly sticky torso I sat back at the desk. "How long will I be in hospital after the operation?" I asked.

"Three days".

"How long will I need to recover after that?"

He shrugged. "It depends … on how we do the reconstruction, on whether we need to take lymph nodes out, on how well you heal".

CANCER WITHOUT SUBTITLES

It wasn't the answer I wanted but it was a fair one.

-0-

I had almost reached the end of the corridor to leave, when the nurse ran after me to say there were more forms to sign, so please could I wait (again). I'm glad she did. How embarrassing would it have been to get another 'where the hell are you?' phone call.

I sent an update to Himself ('just a bit longer - one more person to see') and opened my kindle to (not) read another chapter of my mystery book. It was fifteen minutes before she collected me again and took me to yet another room with yet another doctor.

In English, he introduced himself and said he had spoken with my doctor about me. I realised later that this must have been the 'friend at Ortona' that Thumper had contacted on my behalf, but at the time I assumed he meant the plastic surgeon. Naturally, he too had another mountain of forms for me to sign, but this man took pains to explain them to me. His English was maybe on a par with my Italian so adequate rather than perfect, but it was way more than good enough. I appreciated him speaking English to me more than I can say. It meant I could relax and actually listen instead of being terrified of missing something.

Even so I can't now remember all the details. I do remember that there were three possible options for how they might do the cuts to my breast - one was called lateral and another called quadrante. I can't remember the third. He said they would hope to do a quadrante and drew a picture to show me how the cuts on a quadrante were designed to spare the nipple. Spare my nipple? SPARE MY NIPPLE! I hadn't even thought about having to sacrifice a nipple but now he'd mentioned it I realised that, yes I would really like my nipple spared, thank you very much.

"Do you have any more questions?"

"No" I replied, and it was true. I was still in shock from the nipple revelation.

"In that case I need to give you a prescription for the night before".

"I think I already have it…" I started to say, at the exact moment the nurse said, "I think she already has it."

He began to put his pen down and it occurred to me that I had no idea what prescription he had been about to write.

"I mean I think I have it, but only if it's the injection I have to do at 8pm the night before my operation, otherwise I don't". (I was quite proud of myself for getting all that out in Italian)

"It is".

"In that case I do have it".

"And do you know how to do it?"

"I have to inject myself?" I probably sounded a bit squeaky at this point

"Yes. In your stomach".

In my stomach! Eek! I hadn't realised it was in the stomach. That was even worse. He leaned back in his chair and demonstrated for me exactly where the needle should go. I felt sick at just the thought of it and completely unconvinced I'd be able to do it, but I (naturally) smiled and said "Oh thank you. I see, that's fine, I can do that". I was and still am such a wuss.

So that was it. All that was left to do was wait for the telephone call summoning me to surgery.

Oh, and I saw 5 new people that day.

8 COMING OUT

Going public, telling the relatives, stocking up on bras, more Big Scary Machines (with a radioactive bonus) and preparing to 'go under the knife'.

February 20th

When all this cancer business kicked off, I had decided not to tell anybody 'the bad news' until I had a plan of action. I wanted to be able to say, "Oh by the way I've got cancer but don't worry because dot". For the two months since finding the lump I'd found it hard to keep silent because it's always there at the back of your mind. Having a conversation – any conversation without mentioning it felt deceitful. I normally had a parallel conversation in my head that went something like this:

Them: "Hi how are you doing"

Me: "I'm fine" (thinks *Not great actually. I've got cancer*). "How are you?"

Them. "I'm good too. Did you have a good Christmas?"

Me: "Not too bad" *(think: No, it was shit. I spent most of it worrying about having cancer*). "A bit quiet"

Them: "Us too. Can't wait to get back to normal. Let's hope this year's better eh?"

Me: "Yes let's hope so" (thinks: *you have absolutely no idea how much I hope so*)

Most of the time it was not that complicated, it was just a little voice silently screaming "but I have cancer" onto the end of every sentence I spoke out loud.

After the biopsy I'd said that once I had a plan would be time to start telling people. Now that time had arrived, I was really reluctant to say anything to anyone. I kept thinking 'do I really need to?' which was stupid. I could hardly go through the year keeping it a secret. Except a part of me thought maybe I could. With Covid and not being able to travel and everything, maybe I could get away with it.

Once a week I call a friend of mine who lives in France. Today was that day of the week and I decided I would tell her. Now. Apart from needing to tell her it would be a practise run for telling my sister Rhiannon[13] in the UK. And then my brother, Kempton. I needed to tell them because I'd need them to help me keep it a secret from my mother. The reason I needed to keep it a secret from my mother because (a) she was elderly (b) my dad had died not that long ago and (c) my elder sister had died the year before that. Very horribly. Of cancer. I really didn't want my mum to know.

I practised how I was going to announce it. Wait until

---

[13] Names of my family are the only names I haven't changed for anonymity. It seemed a bit pointless.

the end of the conversation? No, I couldn't do that. It would stop me from hearing what she was saying because I'd be too focused on my news. At the beginning? I dunno, it seemed a bit overdramatic and bombshell-ish to me. Maybe I should just wait for the right opportunity? 'Oh yeah', I scolded myself, 'like that's going to happen.' You know what? There is no such thing as the perfect moment to announce you have cancer. Bugger it, I realised I was just going to have to play it by ear. I did decide though, that I needed to reverse the order: instead of saying I had cancer and I was going to have an operation and ending with the words everything would be ok, I'd start with 'I've got some news, and everything will be ok' and then explain what was happening.

Looking back, I'm not sure how much difference it made. Penny was still horrified.

February 21st

My timeline memories on Facebook were really annoying me. They kept reminding me that February was usually holiday time. Stuck in lockdown with nothing but an operation to look forward to, it was like rubbing salt into the wound.

During the day I tried calling my sister in the UK a few times (and before I could lose my nerve) but there was no reply. She called me back in the evening but as we had had a few friends round for drinks and I was outside a few glasses of wine, I didn't want to tell her. I said I was busy and arranged to talk later in the week.

Instead, I discussed the operation with Himself who wanted to know how I was feeling. The answer was pretty simple: basically, I was frightened of the operation and whatever treatment followed it, but not nearly as frightened as I was of dying. I just wanted to get it over with. This was my third emotional meltdown, but it wasn't as meltdown-y as the first two, so I must have been beginning to adjust.

February 22nd

I was being practical. I would be in hospital three nights which meant at least three pairs of pyjamas with buttons. I emptied out the boxes on top of the wardrobe trying to remember where I might have stored nightwear and eventually discovered I only had two pairs of pyjamas with buttons. I decided they would have to do, even though I was fairly certain they'd be far too warm for a hospital.

February 25th

Sufficiently hyped up at last, I facetimed my sister to tell her 'the news'. Astonishingly she answered the phone on my first attempt but once again I didn't say anything. This time it was because she had the rest of the family there, and all waiting to talk to me. It was pretty much exactly the opposite of the scenario I had planned. And of course, being my family, they all took it in turns to point out what a mess my hair was and how dreadful it looked. Trust me, they really went to town with the criticism. As soon as the call had finished, I messaged my hairdresser and asked for an appointment 'as soon as possible'. Hang the expense. Miserable plus scruffy equalled more miserable.

February 26th

Third time lucky. This time when I phoned Rhiannon it was just her and her partner and so, before I could lose my nerve, I told her what was going on. To my mind, it was going to be harder telling my family than other people because my other sister had died from stomach cancer just a few years ago. It was still very raw so I thought remaining sister would understand why I hadn't said anything before.

That's not her style. Instead I got the third degree on how long 'this' had been going on, and what was the prognosis, interrupted with repeated interjections of 'I can't believe you haven't said anything'. Later on, I got a series of texts from her with all the supplementary questions she forgot to ask. Fortunately, she agreed that we shouldn't breathe a word to mum. There was no point, it would only upset her and there was nothing she could do.

-0-

An Amazon box arrived, containing the white cotton bras I'd ordered for my surgery. They were horrible. Old lady style bras that I'd never look at in a million years under normal circumstances. The only way they could have been worse was if they'd been knicker elastic pink. Even then I'm still not sure.

I had bought two sizes as they seemed to be differently sized to those in the lingerie shop. I was thinking that, if they didn't fit, I'd just have to get some more from a shop. Himself said the nice lingerie shop must have plain white cotton stuff. He was right but I knew that wasn't going into a 'proper' lingerie shop to buy this type of bra This was the type of bra you only wanted to buy anonymously, online.

Grumbling I went to the bedroom and tried them on. One sort of fitted and the other was slightly too big. I figured that if the bigger one was on the tightest band setting it would do and decided to keep both. Presuming my post-op titty would be sore, I might want something looser to cuddle it.

-0-

In bed about to sleep I got a message from my sister. It said she had been rallying all the dead relatives and had some healing to send me ...

Rhiannon: I've just put you in a dome it is lovely all gold & sparkly!! Oh and your house is going to be crowded as I've just called in the clan - that's both nan & paps, Uncle Harry, dad & Nadine. I told them they've all got to go to Italy & give you as much support you need so it is gonna be pretty busy there. Soz lol !! Xx

Me: Great. So they all get a holiday in Italy at my expense!!!

Rhiannon: Well you have to dangle a carrot to get that lot to do anything. Lol. yes it is lovely it is not a normal dome it very elaborate & has a large soft velvet green chair you're all curled up & comfy warm & toasty in it the gold glitter is swirling all around you - that's the healing bit!!

I pictured my dome and imagined myself in the chair. I went to sleep with little bits of gold glitter coming to rest on my eyelids.

February 27th

I had my hair cut. I had it cut really short and changed the colour. It took 4 hours. I loved it but had nowhere to go and no-one to show it off to. Lockdown sucked.

By now, Rhiannon had told Kempton my news, so he phoned me. Gratifyingly he told me that he almost (note the

95

almost) felt sorry for being so horrible about my scruffy hair.

February 28th

I woke up convinced I'd get the call in four days' time, on Thursday. It was spooky.

March 1st

So much for my powers of premonition. The call came three days ahead of my psychic schedule. It told me I had to take a Covid test at Ortona hospital at 9am on Friday, then go and have something done to my lymph nodes at 8.30am in Chieti the following Tuesday. On Tuesday night I should use my first injection from my packet of syringes and then (finally) I had to be at Ortona hospital for the operation at 7am Wednesday.

I wrote a schedule for side of the fridge.

Friday 5 March	09.00	Covid test	Sala conferenza / Ortona
Tuesday 9 March	08.30	Lymph Test	Medicine Nucleare Level 5 Chieti Hospital
Tuesday 9 March	20.00	Injection	Cara at home
Wednesday 10 March	07.00	Operation	Level 4 / Ortona (report to the nurse)

A bit of me was apprehensive but most of me was elated that something was happening. I texted the information to everyone who needed to know.

March 4th

Here's a tip. When you tell yourself you are not worried about something and you just want to get it over with, it's a good idea to tell your subconscious too. Otherwise, all your dreams betray you. After getting my schedule, every night's sleep had been "really shitty". Sorry to swear, but it's the only description that fits.

March 5th

It was the day of the COVID test. 9am in Ortona meant getting up at 7 and leaving by a quarter to 8. At 7.30 a man (unexpectedly) arrived with a delivery of new gravel for our driveway[14]. I started panicking. Himself – more levelheaded - decided that gravel could easily be dumped without supervision and that we should just leave him to it.

The intervention had knocked us off schedule a bit, but we were still there in bags of time. This was great because, as always, after an hours' drive, I was desperate for the loo. After several trips to this hospital, I now knew not only where the toilets were, but which was the best one to use. I was a ninja piddler, and back outside again in less than 5 minutes, where I joined the long queue for Covid Testing.

Testing was in a separate building just to one side of the main hospital, and lower down. The entrance was reached via a

---

[14] Posh description for a gravelled place to park next to the house.

long flight of steps, and this was where everyone was queueing. I was watching what people did, trying to get a clue for myself. Most of them seemed to have forms from somewhere and I didn't have anything. Then a woman came out from the building and said something too fast for me to follow but I managed to catch the word interventi (operations), so I abandoned the queue and ran down the stairs. "Me! Me! I've got an intervento" I panted. "Next Wednesday. I have an appointment".

I'm not sure she understood me, but she took me through anyway. In the entrance hall we went through the doors on the right whereas everyone queuing was being hived off to the doors on the left. Through the doors there was a small curtained off cubicle and she checked my name against a list. I looked over her shoulder and breathed a sigh of relief. I was 3rd down on a list of just 6 people, so I was in the right place. Despite being 3rd I was obviously the first to arrive, but that's what being English does to you. We have an over-developed sense of timekeeping.

There were 4 tables, laid out with sealed packages. She told me to sit down and opened the one that had my name on it. I could see multiple barcodes too. While she was doing this another woman came in and snapped a blue pair of latex gloves over the blue latex gloves she was already wearing. She frowned at me and asked if I spoke Italian. I could tell from her attitude that she wasn't taking any prisoners, so I crossed my fingers and quickly said I did. "Good" she said, "so open your mouth, stick your tongue out and put your head back".

I did as I was told, and she shoved the long taper down the back of my throat. I gagged and gagged and just as I thought I was going to throw up she finished. It would have been a relief if she hadn't moved onto my nostrils which was even worse. That was the third lot of brain matter I'd lost to a Covid swab, and it was only just March. On the plus side I was in and out in less than 5 minutes and we were back on the road by ten past nine.

It would have been earlier if I hadn't had to come out the building by the back entrance whilst himself was waiting by the front. We met back in the car park. Car park meetings were becoming a bit of a theme. This particular car park I liked because it was rarely full and had the ubiquitous hawker 'helpfully' pointing out what spaces were free. This was in sharp contrast to the Chieti car park which was rarely navigable it was so crammed with cars. In Chieti, if a space wasn't available people simply parked at the ends of rows and along the edges of the access.

I digress. It was a beautiful day, almost like an English summer and we drove home on the Guardiagrele route. The last time we had driven this route, just 3 weeks ago, the roads were so iced that sliding and dying seemed a distinct possibility. Today was so blissfully warm we had the windows open.

March 7th

I woke up and looked at the alarm clock. It was ten past four. There was a thought in my head, already fully formed. It told me that if this were 4.10am next Wednesday (the day after tomorrow) I'd be thinking I may as well get up and have my shower. DANG!!! I'm not sure what time the overdrive in my brain switched off and let me go back to sleep but it was well after half past five.

I had a lot of questions and I decided Cristina was the person to ask. I wrote them down and sent her a WhatsApp message.

1. When you arrive with your suitcase do they take you straight to your bed and do you unpack and get undressed and get in and then just wait?

2. Bathrooms? What do you do about showering when you're all bandaged up? How does that work?

3. On the first night do they leave you in the hospital gown to sleep? (Wondering if I need to go and get some more jimjams as I only have 2 pairs).

4. Do you had to stay in bed all day? (assuming I feel up to getting out of it)

5. Do you have to wear a mask the whole time?

She called me back with the name of a local shop where I could buy pyjamas, on account of me having "left it a bit bloody late to thought about that".

Himself sighed, got the car out, and we went shopping.

The shop must have had 50 styles of nightdress (all hateful) and just 5 pairs of women's pyjamas that I also hated on sight. For me, this was old lady bras all over again. I scoured the entire shop for men's pyjamas, but I couldn't find any. With a partial lockdown still in place, going somewhere further afield wasn't an option so I told myself not to be stupid. It was a hospital, not a fashion parade and so what if my pyjamas were awful. Sulkily, I grabbed the least offensive pair and took them to the till.

The assistant had actually rung the price up when Himself spotted the men's pyjamas, right behind me. There was hope! Wait I asked the assistant, can I change my mind? She nodded and I picked a simple blue cotton pair. They were twice as nice and half the price of the ghastly pair I was about to buy. That put me in a good mood for the rest of the day.

March 9th

I woke up thinking 'it's tomorrow'.

I had another feel of the soon to be ex lump in the shower. In the time since I first felt it, it had gone from an 'is it or isn't it' lump to a 'definite' lump. It might have been my imagination but, to me, it had become a really hard mass that you could almost see. I was so pleased it would soon be gone. The rate of change was frightening me. I was also thinking about my lymph nodes. They had been okay so far but there was no reason to suppose they were still clear. Maybe chemotherapy sessions were still in my future. (At this stage I was still labouring under the misapprehension that lymph nodes and chemotherapy were necessarily connected).

-0-

It was pouring with rain when we left and still pouring when we arrived at Chieti. It was 8.15am, the car park was already overflowing with cars, and I needed to be inside by 8.30 so Himself dropped me off outside the main entrance.

Using my medical folder as a ridiculously small umbrella I dashed to the cover of the entrance, paused for the Covid temperature check and ran inside. For some reason I was ridiculously anxious about being late.

I couldn't see directions to Nuclear Medicine at first, but I took several deep breaths and forced myself to look properly. When I looked lower down, I could see paper signs taped to the walls and I followed them. I was glad I wasn't the only person to think the main signage was a bit inadequate.

I walked (trotted) along several corridors and eventually came to the half-glassed door which proclaimed itself to be for Nuclear Medicine. There was a table to the right of the door, holding a box with numbers and instructions to take one and wait. I did.

By 8.27am I was inside the reception area and disinfecting my hands. They checked I was who I said I was, gave me consent forms to sign, gave me another number, and took my file away into an inner office. I was given plastic shoes covers to put on and told to disinfect my hands (again), and finally they took me through to an inner waiting room. There was one person already in there. She looked terrified. I wondered if that was how I looked. I suspect it was.

I sat and waited, pretending to watch the TV and an older woman came out of a connecting room, clutching her bra in her hand. She walked over to her jacket, hanging up on a hook, and stuffed the bra into the jacket pocket. I thought that was a bit odd.

A nurse came out of the same room and called me (or at least my number) to come inside and leave my stuff where it was. It was a windowless room with a semi reclined chair in its' centre, a bit like a dentist chair but larger. This was where I had to sit. A doctor came through another door and introduced himself. He explained that he was about to inject radioactive stuff into the lump in my titty so that 'we' could see how far it travelled. Those were not his exact words you understand but my translation.

I took my top and my bra off, with one eye on the syringe he was preparing. It was horrendous – absolutely massive – and I was astonished when I didn't feel it going in. There was no sensation in the lump at all. I left my bra off and put my top back on as instructed then the nurse took me back to the inner waiting room, where I too stuffed my bra into the pocket of my jacket.

The older woman who had come out before me heard me talking to the nurse and decided I was okay to talk to. The fact that I only understood half of what she said didn't faze her at all, so I had all the usual questions like why was I in Italy, what did I do, did I have children, had I been to Lanciano (her hometown) etc. The terrified looking woman watched us but didn't join in. She was too busy being terrified. Eventually she too was called into the injection room and my chatty companion was collected and taken away for the next stage.

I was on my own, but not for long.

The terrified woman came back out. This time she tried talking to me, but I could tell her heart wasn't in it – she was just trying to distract herself. Nonetheless we limped along making small talk until it was my turn to be collected for the next stage.

-0-

My next room had a Big Scary Machine in it. Not quite as Big and Scary as the MRI machine but nonetheless Big and Scary enough for me. Under instruction, I took the dressing (tampone) off from the injection site and lay on the moving bed part of the Big Scary Machine, with one arm lifted over my head. The bed moved and the plate overhead came down. I made the mistake of opening my eyes and immediately shut them again. The massive plate was about an inch away from me. It was instant claustrophobia.

After a while (and a lot of Big Scary Machine noises) the plate went up and the nurse came back into the room. I hadn't finished. This was just to reposition me on another table. This position was more uncomfortable because I was on my side by with my arm still stretched over my head. She kept saying ferma[15] and I was thinking what does she want me to sign, but then she said, in English, 'stop' and I realised she had been telling me to stay still. All those signatures (firma) I'd done had addled my brain.

I couldn't properly see what was happening, but she was dragging something across my skin that made Geiger-counter type noises, then making marks on me with a permanent marker. I could see it was a permanent marker from the corner of my eye. She repeated the process a few times, going in and out of the room to consult with the doctor/operator in the control room. Control room probably isn't the right terminology but that's what it seemed like.

Then it was finished. I was told I couldn't shower as the marks on my skin were needed for the surgeon, and I was given the report I needed to hand over the next day. It was in a sealed envelope. Bummer.

---

[15] Firma and ferma sound identical to my English ear. it was like me saying beer and bear to an Italian, They can't hear the difference.

Someone escorted me to the door where I had to take the plastic shoes covers off and disinfect my hands again, and I was free to go. By ten past nine I was back in the hospital reception and Himself was picking me up.

Evening

Himself checked my packing for the hospital. I was a bit (actually a lot) miffed because I was and am, an expert packer. In my small weekend case I had four pairs of pyjamas – one for each night and an extra in case, underwear for four days, a pair of Birkenstocks (I don't own slippers), the two horrible white cotton bras and some clothes to come home in. To this I'd added nine satsumas and some biscuits in case the food was too horrible to eat, a bottle of water, my iPad and kindle, chargers, spectacles, Cara's dining set, a wash bag and a towel. It was already full, but I was confident I could squeeze my bathrobe in.

I undressed in the bathroom and looked at the marks in my armpit. Presumably those were the lymph nodes that would be going.

I washed my hair in the sink as I wouldn't be able to wash the next day, and if I didn't wash it, it was going to be rank by Saturday.

At 8pm promptly, Cara arrived to give me the first injection. Being injected in the stomach is nasty. My level of squeamishness was not boding well for what was to come.

9 THE OPERATION

**More pink rooms, another ultrasound, making a new
friend, finding McPherson, becoming French, the inside
view of an operating theatre, experiencing hospital food
and coming out with a 'nice job'.**

March 10th

I woke up at 2.30am. I think I must had dozed after but when
the alarm went off at 5am I was already awake and it felt like I
hadn't slept at all. I couldn't stop yawning.

My bathrobe (all washed and lovely for the hospital)
refused to be crammed into my case so Himself loaned me his
unwashed but less bulky one. So now I had a man's bathrobe,
men's' pyjamas and Birkenstocks in place of slippers. Hmmm.

The cats were our only witnesses when we left at
5.45am. Given that I'd had only a flannel wash and had no
make-up on, that was probably a good thing.

-0-

At 6.45am we arrived at the hospital. Gulp. This was it. Himself couldn't come in with me so we shared a long hug outside. Then another. And another, for luck. Inside, I walked my suitcase up the stairs to the 4th floor. It took longer that way and I was in no hurry.

The 4th floor had a large waiting area lined with plastic seats, about a quarter full with people. It was as far as you could go because the door to the ward area was secured, so I sat down to wait. I was alone. Nobody else was. Everyone else had completely ignored the instructions to arrive unaccompanied and was sitting with at least one other person. Some were with three or four. Stripping out the assorted family and friends I thought there were about 5 of us in for an actual operation. Or maybe more, I don't know.

I was checked in at 7am promptly and taken through the locked doors onto the ward. I can't describe much of it because we were confined to our rooms for most of the time, but the door led to a corridor with a series of patient rooms on the right-hand side. I recall the nurses' station being on the left. I think the kitchen area was also on the left. 'My room' was about halfway along the corridor, on the right, directly opposite the nurses' station which is why I remember it being there.

The room was generously sized with three beds and its own large bathroom. By the window, with its view of the distant sea, there was a small dining table with two chairs. Only two chairs I later realised because only two of the beds were occupied. It was, of course, painted pink. Whoever decided all things breast cancer should be pink has a lot to answer for.

Across the room the chatty woman from Lanciano was being given instructions by a nurse. We smiled at each other in that 'yes I've recognised you too' sort of way. Then I concentrated on my own nurse and my instructions. They weren't difficult. Unpack our things into our wardrobe and get into our pyjamas straight away. So, that was that Cristina question answered.

Unpacking I discovered a little (soft toy) cat secreted in my suitcase. He looked like Campbell, one of my home cats. I sent a 'what's this?' text to Himself and he told me that the home cats had sent him to keep me company. He was called McPherson. McPherson was slightly boss eyed - much like I felt. I put him on top of my cabinet facing me.

-0-

Feeling well underdressed in my new pyjamas I sat on the bed and waited for whatever happened next. What happened was a nurse arrived and shaved my armpit that I shaved just two days before. There was literally no hair there to shave. Then another arrived with more forms to sign and another list of questions, like existing medications and so on (none). I handed over my sealed envelope from the day before. She glanced at the contents but said nothing, which was a bit frustrating.

I carried on waiting, staring into space and wondering if I shouldn't be doing something else but what else was there to do? After a little while a nurse came in and beckoned me off the bed. "Put your robe on and come with me". I did. She took me back to the ward's security door. "Wait here." She disappeared into another wardroom and re-emerged, walking very slowly, with an old lady leaning on her arm. How old I didn't know but I estimated early 90s. Taking fairy steps I followed them through the doors to the lift, down a floor, and then to the virulently pink waiting room with the bookcase and the children's' colouring sheets.

Once again, I was told to wait, and the nurse took the old lady into a consulting room. I checked the books. No change. Once again, I sat on a chair and stared into space trying to look unconcerned. Once again, after only a few minutes alone I was wondering if maybe I'd misunderstood what I'd been told. What if I wasn't supposed to wait there indefinitely? What if they forgot I was there? How long should I give it before I went to find someone and ask them?

I was still dithering when the nurse brought the old lady back. Phew. She told me to go into the examination room and she'd come back for me later. It turned out I was having another ultrasound. From somebody who had had precisely one ultrasound in her entire life, I was sure making up for it now.

The completed ultrasound was compared with my previous tests and the results added to my file. That's my file that the medics had, rather than my file that I had, now in the drawer beside my hospital bed just in case. I was fitted with an identity bracelet and the nurse returned to escort me upstairs again. I thought this was a bit unnecessary: I could easily had walked back on my own. Much as I wanted to run away, I wasn't about to make a break for it.

-0-

The nurse commented that I was her first French patient when we arrived back at my bed. I said I wasn't French.

She looked at me. "Are you sure?" she said. I promised her I was.

My roommate was also back so we introduced ourselves formally. Her name was Claudia. Just like the day before, she spoke incredibly fast, and I was floundering after just a few sentences. I asked her to slow down, and she did, but after a few minutes she forgot and was back to machine gun delivery. I gave up and just did the best I could. It did get easier over the time we were there. I think I moved from 20% comprehension to a full 50% at times.

Claudia was (still is) is the perfect nonna and instantly appointed herself as my stand in mama. She also, amusingly, appointed herself as my explainer, saying "she's foreign and won't understand you" to anyone who came into the room. I particularly loved it when she telephoned her daughter and told her that I seemed very nice, but it was a real bummer I was English because it meant she couldn't really chat with me (my translation). Trust me, my lack of understanding was no barrier to her chatting.

I lapsed into the twilight zone that was hospital time.

-0-

Eventually two people arrived with a gurney and told me it was time to go. I'd put my phone in the drawer along with my rings and jewellery, so I had no real idea what time it was. Lunchtime-ish maybe? Did it really matter? No, but I'd have liked to know.

I took my pyjamas off and replaced them with the gown they gave me, then scooted myself onto the trolley and watched the ceiling pass by as we went along the corridor to a wide-doored lift. This was it.

The lift, they told me, would take us straight down to the operating theatre. While we were inside one asked if I was French or English (what was this French thing?). I replied that I was English. Well, that was it ... "Why was I in Italy? Did I know London?" When I told them that yes, I had lived in London for years they came back with "No!!! Really? What on earth are you doing in Abruzzo?". This reaction is something I encounter often, especially amongst younger people who see London as a glittering metropolis. They simply can't believe anyone would swap the bright lights of London for sleepy old Abruzzo. I rhapsodised over the food, the weather and the people but I could tell my escorts still thought London for Abruzzo was a por exchange. The brownie points I got from living in London were snatched away because of my poor judgement in leaving it.

Out of the lift we were in something that wasn't a waiting room but wasn't exactly a theatre either. It was a sort of operating theatre annexe if there is such a thing. Here we stopped and I was handed over to another two people who fitted me with a canula and carefully explained the process of anaesthesia. They took my face mask away and gave me a proper one. It was very substantial which was just as well as I was going to be in a mask for the foreseeable future.

I was expecting to do that counting backwards from a hundred thing before we went inside and, if I was honest, it was worrying me a bit. It would be harder in Italian. While they carried on talking to each other, too fast for me to follow, I tuned them out and started practising in my head. Then the words "here we go" got through my filter and I braced myself. I was all ready with my un cento, novanta nove, novant'otto but …. no, they wheeled me straight into the operating theatre without a countdown.

The operating theatre was a large room with massive lights. From my supine position I could see a cluster of trolleys and equipment in the centre. I was wheeled into the centre of these. I'd never consciously been in an operating theatre before and the very small part of me that wasn't completely clenched up with fear was fascinated. I was drinking it all in when they began to attach things to me and suddenly – zilch - I was gone. My next memory was being shifted back into my bed in the room.

-0-

I dozed, woke, dozed and woke. I was conscious of a cold thing tucked under my arm, but it wasn't uncomfortable. After a while I realised it was an ice pack. At one point I vaguely registered Claudia being taken away for her operation. I dozed some more, woke up and felt conscious enough to read a book for a while. A doctor visited and examined me, but I wasn't sure which one it was. I dozed again. Claudia returned and I watched them making her comfortable. At some stage I sent Himself a text to tell him was done and I was awake. He was amazed. Later, when I saw that I had sent that message at 2.45pm, so was I.

At dinner time I was expected to get out of bed and sit at the table to eat. 'Seriously?' I thought. I mumbled something about not being hungry, but nobody was having any truck with that nonsense. I had to eat, and I had to get out of bed to do it. I did as I was told and got out of bed.

Something I hadn't seen was at the side of the bed and it almost made me stumble. That's when I first realised I had a drain attached to me. I was such a medical newbie that it hadn't occurred to me. The nurse showed me the bag I had been given to carry it in and fitted it across my shoulder for me. It was actually quite a nice bag in dark blue cloth and designed to be the perfect strap length. I came to be quite attached to that bag in the end, and not just literally.

I got to the table and lowered myself gingerly to the chair. In front of me was a plastic tray with a bowl of liquid something, and plastic wrapped, disposable cutlery. It seemed that Covid had superseded the need for Cara's tablecloth and cutlery. "It's Brodino" the nurse told me. "Eat".

I'd heard of Brodino but never had it and now I know why. Brodino is a light broth, so flavourless it would make water taste interesting. It looks boring, it tastes boring and the effort it took to eat it was extraordinary. As I lifted my right arm it shook, and the shaking multiplied the higher I tried to lift. I dipped the spoon into the Brodino, raised it, and the Brodino splashed straight out again. I compromised by bending my head down to meet the spoon, but my hand shook so much I still spilled half before it got to my mouth. I think it took me 25 minutes to swallow a third of the bowl of Borodino and it exhausted me.

I went back to bed and read my book. Claudia was now awake, so we chatted, or rather I listened while she talked. She told me all about her family and I asked her to slow down every second sentence and repeat every forth word. We were interrupted several times by nursing staff checking on us which gave my poor brain a respite from translation. Nonetheless I learned that her husband had died 3 years ago, and that she had three children, one of whom spent a year in London. She also had four grandchildren aged 9,7, 3 and a brand new one. She showed me photographs of everyone. She showed me the get-well card one of her grandchildren had made.

Eventually Claudia tired of talking to me and needed to rest. I picked my phone and started texting people to tell them where I was. This time I didn't worry about how to phrase things so a few of my friends got a bit of a shock when they read their phones.

Operation Day plus one: March 11th

The day started early. We were woken at 5.30 and checked over. More nurses appeared to do things to us. Injections, dressing checks, drainage checks. I forget exactly what. "Bonjour" said one brightly to me before I had even opened my mouth. I smiled back at her. "I'm not French, I'm English". She seemed disappointed.

By 6.30am we were out of our beds and the bedding was changed at 7. I was back on (not in) my bed at 8 when I accidentally pulled my cannula from my wrist. The fountain of blood that shot out of me was impressive even if I say so myself. So was their reaction. The flow of blood was stemmed, and my bedding completely changed inside ten minutes. As a bonus (for me) they decided not to replace the canula.

For breakfast I was asked if I wanted coffee, tea or Orzo. I didn't really want coffee and Italian tea was not to be contemplated. Claudia told me that Orzo was lovely, so I chose that. That was the last time I took Claudia's advice on beverages. Orzo was a bowl of something vaguely but not actually coffee-ish that you apparently dunk dry bready-type biscuits into. Disgusting is the politest way I could describe it.

After breakfast it was time for an injection and more blood pressure/pulse rate/ice bag/fluid drain checks and then I was told to put on my dressing gown as we were going to see 'the surgeon'. The nurse walked me the short distance to a small consulting room within the ward and I lay down on the slightly elevated table inside it. The surgeon – the lovely woman with the smiley face - took the dressing carefully off of my chest.

"Ooh" she said, looking sideways at it. "Ooh". She leaned over to look me in the face "Nice job!".

I squinted down – I couldn't see much apart from a lot of orange-stained skin, but I could see that I still had a nipple and that was enough. I was elated.

As if that wasn't enough good news, she then told me I could go home tomorrow. It was healing well, and I didn't need to stay in a third night.

-0-

When Claudia came back from her check she had also been told she could go home. She immediately took out her phone and called her family. There were a lot of them to call. Then she called her friends. Then the people who weren't there when she called them, called her back. It was a lot of calling. She told them all about me too. I know this because she looked at me when she was doing it and I kept catching the word inglese amongst the torrent of fast Italian. But I also caught the words "molto gentile", so I knew she wasn't saying anything horrible.

While Claudia was talking I changed back into my pyjamas, read my kindle, sent texts, and watched tv on my iPad. Whenever Claudia had a break between phone calls she talked to me, telling me more about the people in her family, introducing me to some of them via Facetime. As we became friendlier, she shared her favourite videos of the Pope with me, and I told her that himself's (now deceased) uncle had helped organise Pope John Paul's UK tour many moons ago. That was the 'Kissing the Tarmac' tour. She was very impressed; so impressed that she wanted me to see and hold something her granddaughter had given her to 'keep her safe'. I was not sure entirely what it was, but it was clearly a religious charm. I was reminded of the religious relics I used to read about in history lessons. I would have asked her if it was something to do with relics, but my Italian wasn't up to the translation. And anyway, it was enough for me to simply exclaim "che bella".

-0-

More nurses came in and out during the day. A few asked me about my French ancestry. When I denied it they complimented me on my Italian. From that I gathered that French people speak Italian better than we English. I don't know if it's true or not, but it wouldn't surprise me. Italian isn't the easiest language in the world to learn. Not that I've learnt anything else, other than French and that only very badly.

-0-

The highlight of the day was the food. Given my Brodino experience and the dire warnings I'd been given, the food was a revelation. Lunch was pasta, spinach, melanazane parmigiana and a mandarin to follow. Dinner was equally good. It was streets ahead of the food my father used to have when I visited him in hospital, and I concluded that Italian patients are a lot fussier than their British counterparts. Claudia certainly complained that the portions were 'mean' (they weren't) and thought it was 'ridiculous' that they only served water, not wine.

-0-

After dinner Claudia suggested a passeggiata up and down the corridor and I agreed to join her. She looped her hand through my arm for balance and we stepped outside the room. We were busted within three seconds. No, we were told. We could not walk in the corridor. Had we forgotten about Covid? Feeling like chastened 5-year-olds we went back inside where Claudia crept around and round the room until she was satisfied she'd (a) had enough exercise, and (b) more importantly, made her point. I think she may have been quite a rebellious 5-year-old.

I of course, have never rebelled in my life[16]. Ceding her the floor space I retired back to my bed and my book. Don't ask me what I was reading. I've no idea.

-0-

I ought to tell you about the pain. It was fine. In fact, the lack of pain was remarkable. Yes, of course there was some pain, but it was more in the discomfort range than anything else. It was so mild that I happily refused the extra pain medication offered. In the entire day I took just one extra

---

[16] Yes, that is a total lie.

tablet, and that was shortly before bedtime. If I hadn't been so incredibly weak and wobbly and slow when I moved, I would have felt almost normal.

Going Home Day March 12th

The day started at 5.30am with health checks. This time I was compos mentis enough to remember what they were. First there was a finger prick, then a temperature check and finally they examined the drain and changed the bottle. We went back to sleep and were woken again at 7.15. This time when they asked if I had pain I said yes and I was given an injection. The initial medication was clearly wearing off.

Breakfast arrived. I thought I'd be smart and chose coffee this time. It was still disgusting.

After breakfast Claudia had her canula taken out. Her drain had been removed the night before and I was deeply envious. I really wanted mine gone too because I kept forgetting it and had already yanked it several times. We'd only known each other two days but Claudia already knew me well enough to yell "borsa!" at me every time I moved from the bed. Borsa is Italian for bag and in this case, also shorthand for 'don't forget to pick your drain up and put it in the shoulder bag you dozy cow'.

They took Claudia away to have her final check from the surgeon and I pottered around, not knowing what to do with myself. I knew I was going home, but to pack before I'd been examined seemed a bit previous. Mainly I just gazed through the window at the distant sea and wondered how cold it was outside.

Claudia came back and it was my turn. The process was the same as the day before but with a more hands-on examination of the wound site. They told me they were happy; that it was a lovely job and they cleaned and re-dressed my breast. I was given a date for a check-up appointment and reminded that I had to inject myself once a day in the morning until I ran out of the prescribed syringes. I pointed to the drain and said "…is this?" but they pre-empted my question saying I had to keep it for a while. The shoulder bag was mine for the duration.

-0-

Back in the room Claudia was dressed and almost packed. She was as thrilled as me to be heading home and invited me to visit her in Lanciano 'when all this was over'. She was bubbling with information "When is your next appointment? Oh, that's the same day as me, we might will see each other then. Is your husband on his way? No? I've already called my daughter; she's coming to pick me up". Finally, she wound down. "But you need to call your husband to fetch you and you need to pack" she said, "and I need to call some people and tell them I'm coming home".

To the background of Claudia calling everyone on her extensive list of friends and family I got my suitcase out. Of the four pairs of pyjamas I had brought with me I had worn only the blue cotton pair, and those only for one night. The bathrobe and Birkenstocks were both worn, the wash flannel and towel were both used and that was it. The satsuma, the biscuits and bottle of water were untouched, Cara's dining set was unused and there was no way I could put even the bigger of the horrible white cotton bras on my body. I repacked the case as best I could with only one arm and sat on the case to get it closed.

-0-

Lunch arrived just as Claudia was leaving. She and I both refused even though it looked delicious. The man delivering the lunches told me that everyone was leaving today and that was unusual. It looked like there were going to be a lot of wasted lunches.

I sat on my bed, alone and waited. We were not allowed to leave the locked ward until our transport home had arrived. When Himself rang to say he was waiting outside the hospital I told him he could come up to the 4th floor to meet me. I know the instructions said don't, but everybody else was being met inside, so I didn't see why I should be any different.

As we were only ten minutes behind Claudia she was still in the hospital, just outside the ward. I was welcomed like she hadn't just said goodbye a few minutes ago and introduced to her daughter. I introduced Himself in return and she treated him to a blast of the same rapid-fire Italian I'd been experiencing for the past few days. He looked shell shocked. He had thought I was exaggerating.

Then we made our slow progress to the car park, and I very delicately inserted myself into the back seat. For the first time in over 50 hours, I took my mask off properly. I'll be honest, it was a relief.

Using a seat belt was out of the question so I sat in the back of the car for the journey home. The last part of our journey, over the deeply potholed local roads, were a special kind of hell. Himself drove as slowly and carefully as possible while I tried to protect my breast against the jolting, but every bump was agony. When we got home, I swore that I was not going out in the car again until I absolutely had to.

10 POST-OP RECOVERY

Flowers and treats, more horrible bras, the first check-up, moving my arm again, the second check-up, my first proper shower and friends indeed.

Home

The next few days were a blur. People arrived with flowers, pampering gifts and goodwill messages. I could not do anything much with my right arm, so I ate the biscuits, saved the body creams for later and admired the pre-vased, beautifully arranged flowers. For the most part I got up, moved to the settee, stayed there all day watching Netflix ad nauseum, then moved back to bed. In between I ate and slept. Himself was doing EVERYTHING and all those cookery programmes he likes to watch were paying off big time.

Sleeping at night was an issue. Himself had vacated our bed for the duration, so I could sleep with the luxury of space, and without fear of joggling but it was still a palaver. Every bedtime I would place the wound drain to one side, lay the tube carefully in position and then build a nest of pillows to keep myself and my recuperating breast in one place. I was sleeping on my back, which I hardly ever do, so every time I fell asleep my body instinctively wanted to turn. If I did move, the pain would wake me up instantly. I hated being alone and, although I slept deeply when I slept, the nights seemed very long.

Every morning I had a painfully slow strip wash and injected myself in my tummy. Knowing my squeamishness with needles, three people had offered to do it for me but I didn't feel I could ask people to come to my house every day. Himself offered too but I declined. I knew he'd be so hesitant and worried about hurting me that he'd end up doing just that.

No, the only way was to face up to it and do it slowly, with steely determination. It did get easier with time, although no less unpleasant. I had to choose a new site each day and soon had a line of bruises across my stomach showing where I'd been. After a week the colours were a good indication of how long ago each injection was.

March 15th

3 days after getting home I was about to get in the car and face the potholed roads again. Much as I hated the idea it was clear that just two horrible white cotton bras were not going to see me through the next weeks. I needed to buy some more, and I remembered the pyjama shop selling something similar. I was pretty sure I'd seen plain white cotton bras, and I was certain they'd be a lot cheaper than the horrors I had bought online. We were going there.

The shop was almost empty. Just an assistant and two customers. The assistant was tied up with one of them, so I started searching through the displays myself, looking for the right size. Himself initially hung back but eventually started to rummage too. I found underwired bras in my size but no bras without underwire. That figures I thought.

I was about to give up when the assistant came over. I told her what I was looking for and she started rummaging as well. That was three of us.

The other customer, hearing my voice, turned around. "Hey, ciao, come stai?" she said to me, and I recognised the mother of a girl I know. She clocked my drain bag. "Che ha successo?" (What happened) she asked.

"I've, um, had an operation" I said, vaguely gesturing at my right breast. "That's why I need a bra".

"What size do you need?" She joined the search. That was four of us.

Despite the collective effort we were, ultimately, unsuccessful. The mother suggested I buy a bra and take the wires out. The assistant said that was a good idea and she'd do it for me. I said no to both. I'd decided I'd just have to get another horrible internet jobbie. We departed the shop with much virtual hugging and good wishes for my fast healing. Predictably, her daughter was on the phone within an hour. So now the whole of Casoli knew about my operation too[17].

March 16th

Wearing my horrible white cotton also slightly big too old lady bra I went back to Ortona for a wound check-up. We drove, as

---

[17] I'm exaggerating, I only know about 4 people in Casoli.

was now customary, with me in the back seat like Lady Muck, clutching my right titty against any potential jolting. It was a really boring way to travel, but this time it was only one way. That's because they took the drainage tube out. Oh, the bliss. Well worth the bizarre sensation of feeling something being suctioned from inside then slithered outside from your body. It wasn't painful but it definitely caused a little bit of vomit to rise up in my throat and be swallowed back down.

I asked about next steps and I thought they said I would be told at my next appointment, which was disappointing but not tragic. It was only another week to wait. What really mattered was that I was down to one small dressing and could travel home sitting in the front of the car. I still had to hold the seat belt away from and clutch my titty whenever we reached a pot-holed bit but hell, that was nothing.

March 17th

Now the drainage tube was out it was time to start arm exercises in earnest. I had downloaded a list of exercises from Cancer Research UK a few days after I got back and thought they looked incredibly easy. That was before I started.

As soon as I started, I discovered that lifting my arm out to the side and up was ridiculously painful and carrying anything heavier than a cup of tea was nigh on impossible. I began with shoulder shrugs and gradually moved on to actual arm movements. It said that after about two weeks was the right time to start these. It also said that I could had sex if I didn't lift my arms above my shoulders. Seriously? I was still sharing my bed with a mountain of pillows holding me in position and nothing more than a stuffed toy cat to cuddle. Sex seemed like something that only happened to an alien species on another planet right now.

March 19th

At my second wound check-up in Ortona I bumped into Claudia. She was doing well. I hadn't realised that she had been taking oral chemotherapy before her operation so, whilst I was still at the beginning, this was one of the last stages for her. I was nervous, thinking that today would be the day I would hear about my next treatments.

Almost as soon as I got inside the consulting room I was once again half stripped and laying on the couch. The doctor took off the dressing ("ooh, nice job") snipped off all the remaining bits of stitching, had a feel around and said the dressing could stay off. He said everything was looking good and they would call me to come in again in around a week's time.

I plucked up my courage and asked what my next treatment was and when, but he said they didn't yet have the histology results. They apparently needed these before deciding. I could only assume that my lump was sitting in a lab somewhere, still being examined. I felt frustrated, and desperate to know what was coming next. Even if it was awful (think chemo) I just wanted to know.

That evening I braced myself. There comes a point where you actually have to look at yourself in a mirror and this was it. I was dreading it.

You know what? It was okay. I mean yes, there was a livid scar right across the side of my breast, but I knew that would fade in time. What mattered was that the operated-on breast looked, for all intents and purposes, the same as the unoperated-on breast. I assumed this must all be down to the skill of the plastic surgeon. Nice job.

March 20th

Dressing free, I could swap the strip wash for a shower. I also discovered that if I bent right over and took frequent rests, I could use the hairdryer. Next step would be lifting the kettle (so long as it was almost empty).

March 21st

I took a photo of my scar. For the next 6 months I took a photo every four weeks so I could see the progress. Don't worry. I'm not sharing them.

March 24th

I moved onto the lifting the arm up exercises. If I walked my fingers up the wall I could get my arm to slightly below elbow height.

By now I was in regular text conversation with friends in the UK who'd had their own cancer experiences. To anybody going through cancer treatment I really do recommend talking to people who have been through it. Especially people you already know. It's brilliant for getting a heads up on what's coming next. Plus, you get a heap of hands-on advice that isn't published on any web sites.

March 28th

A good day. It was my wedding anniversary and warm enough to sit outside for a while. I had flowers. In fact, I had two lots of flowers because the Interflora equivalent here screwed up the order and 2 florists delivered. I wasn't complaining.

March 29th

Cara was still checking up on me, despite working so hard and being so tired that she told me she had driven up onto the pavement driving home. I told her I was still waiting to hear about the histology.

11 EXPECTATIONS AND INVITATIONS

Scaring the neighbours, my first oncology clinic, my first CUP, a treatment schedule and the moving target that is radiotherapy,

April 3rd

Finally, at my 3rd post operative check-up at Ortona (it all looked excellent by the way) I was given information on what would be happening next. it was not a treatment plan - I had an appointment at Chieti hospital the following Tuesday to get that - but it was an indication of what to expect. The recommendation was for tablets and radiotherapy. Brilliant! I thought. No chemotherapy! The relief was profound.

I also had an email address to make an appointment for integrated care (Medicine Integrata) which I thought was all about looking after yourself type-stuff: exercise, foods, all that kind of thing. The surgeon said the programme was not compulsory, but it was very good, so I decided to give it a go.

April 4th

Re-reading the report and recommendations I had been given I noticed that the radiotherapy was listed for a hospital in Teramo. I didn't know Teramo. I looked up Teramo. It was 2 hours away. I told Cara and she said that was ridiculous. When I went to Chieti, I should ask to have it changed.

April 5th

Walking was my only possible exercise, so I tried to go out daily. As I walked, I kept lifting my arm out to the side and up, as far as I could. Out, up, down. Out, up, down. Out, up, down. It killed two exercise birds with one stone. It also generated some very suspicious looks from other people.

April 6th

Back in Chieti hospital but this time on an upper floor and in a different wing. Fortunately, I'd left myself a ridiculous amount of time to find the oncology department and, after only one false start, I was sitting in yet another hospital waiting room. I was also about half an hour early. It was deserted and the reception desk was closed for lunch.

I selected a seat in the middle row and sat there, pretending to read a book whilst actually worrying that I was in the wrong place. As the time of my appointment drew closer and the room remained empty, I become more and more convinced I was in the wrong place. I was calculating whether I had time to go back to the main hospital reception and ask when another person came in. Then another. And another.

The reception desk opened and immediately closed again. Somebody went in through the barriered doors. Somebody came out of the barriered doors and spoke to one of the people waiting. My appointment time had been and gone. I moved from my seat in row 4 to the middle of row 1 and the next time the door opened I was ready. I sprang forward clutching my piece of paper with my appointment. "Was I in the right place?" I asked. They studied my bit of paper and said yes. I just need to wait until I was called.

Reassured I sat down and the clawing anxiety in my stomach went away. Well, the clawing anxiety about being in the wrong place went away. The clawing anxiety about having a cancer consultation in a foreign language was still very much there. That particular anxiety never went away, just ebbed and flowed with my appointment schedule.

Eventually it was my turn. A woman came out through the doors, snapped out my name and immediately turned on her heel to go inside again. I almost dropped everything getting to the door before it swung shut behind her. She strode along a featureless corridor and then another, with me trotting to keep up beside her. She stopped outside a room and nodded me inside. "In here" she said. Apart from my name it was the only thing she said.

-0-

The office was small, mercifully painted green not pink, and dominated by a large desk. Two women sat behind it, one older (clearly the doctor) and one younger (a junior doctor I think). For ease, they are henceforth called Senior and Junior. They asked my name and I gave it, followed by my date of birth. At every appointment I had been asked my date of birth

131

as an added check and now I said it automatically. There was a chair in front of the desk, and I went to sit down. Before I could Senior pointed to a second chair, against the far wall. 'No. Sit there'. It wasn't a good start. Sitting that far away would make it harder to follow what they were saying, especially with masks on. Plus, my crap hearing that I've failed to mention so far.

While I sat in silence, they studied my notes on a computer then opened a huge file (mine) and began to read through it. They asked if I was happy with the results of the operation. I said yes. There was more silence as they carried on reading. I used the opportunity to ask about radiotherapy. Specifically, radiotherapy in Teramo.

Two hours away was ridiculous they said. Where do you live? I told them. Then I told them where it was near. Then I told them the nearest town of any size at all and this one they finally recognised. They decided that the staff in Ortona must have confused my Civitella with another, different Civitella and I really should have the treatment in Chieti. Senior picked up the phone to call the radiotherapy department but the person she needed to speak to wasn't there. 'Don't worry' she said. 'Leave it with me and I'll fix it'.

Senior put the phone down and returned to studying the computer. She and Junior discussed dates for my next visit and Junior went off to check availability. While Junior was gone, Senior quizzed me about my experience in Ortona. Like Cara she was keen to impress upon me that it was a centre of excellence, and I could not have been in better hands. I agreed with her.

'Now we need to talk about next steps' she said. 'This' (she printed off a sheet of paper) is a list of the tests you must have, and then we will decide on the treatment'.

Uh oh. This wasn't what I was expecting.

'I thought it was just radiotherapy I'm having?'

"No" she replied, 'it may be chemotherapy too. We won't know until we have more results from the laboratory. While we wait these are the tests you must have'.

I was so crushed by this news I wanted to cry. I felt sick. I took the sheet of paper she was holding out and read it. It looked like I was being tested for everything they could throw at me. According to this list I would be spending pretty much all of the next week in Chieti and Ortona.

There was a pen on the desk, so I stood up to take it. I needed to made notes on the list. Without thinking I sat down in the forbidden (by the desk) chair to write but this time they let me stay there. Although I noticed they silently nudged the hand sanitiser my way.

I scribbled her supplementary instructions all over the list of tests, signed more consent forms and put the pen back on the desk. Senior ostentatiously disinfected it. Finally, I was given me more prescriptions (ricette) and told I had to take them to the CUP. Slight problem. I didn't know what a CUP was. She told me that a CUP is where the appointments are made and in this hospital it was on the 5th floor near radiology. That was a stroke of luck. I knew where radiology was, and actually now remembered seeing signs that said CUP.

After this I could go. I came out of the room and, for a moment, froze. I hadn't taken anything in on my way there and had no idea where to go. Logically I should have stuck my head back inside the door and asked which way to go, If I had been back in the UK that's exactly what I would have done but here it was all part and parcel of being out of my depth. I didn't want to admit defeat. Turning left seemed best so I did. Fortunately, I was right, although the corridors were so long that I wasn't sure until I actually saw the door in front of me.

-0-

I went straight to the other hospital wing and found the CUP on the 5th floor. It was a massive room with multiple glassed in, numbered booths around the edges and a lot of people standing in socially distanced islands in the centre. There was an electronic display board with a series of differently coloured letters and numbers that changed as I watched. A240 – 2 , C26 - 4, D49 - 1, B2 - 8. There seemed to be no logic to it, but as the numbers changed people would move to a booth that matched the second number.

I watched to see what other newcomers did when they came in. They all went to a machine that looked a little like a dispenser for railway tickets, pressed a button and took a ticket. I went to look at it too. Now I could see that the colours and letters of the alphabet related to the category of tickets that people took. One colour/letter was for people with disabilities, another for expectant mothers, families and so on. I pressed the button that seemed to say something like 'just an ordinary patient' and took the ticket that came out.

Holding my ticket, I watched the board until my number and colour appeared and went to the desk indicated. I was feeling quite smug about how well I was navigating this new hurdle as I handed over my bundle of ricette and my list.

The woman looked at me, looked at my ricette and barked a question. I didn't understand a word. She repeated it and I realised she was giving me a date. 'Yes, that's right' I said without having a clue why I said it. I had no idea what the significance of the date was. She frowned, nodded, bashed some computer keys, printed out more bits of paper and handed everything back to me. I was done. I later discovered that I'd given her an extra riccetta in error and had managed to book myself in for the same procedure twice. Worse, they were in Ortona and Chieti respectively and on two different dates. I was clearly being nowhere near as smart as I thought I was.

April 7th

According to my list I had to arrange blood tests. I had the ricetta for these but no idea how to actually do it. I texted Cara for help and she said to go to the CUP at Casoli hospital or call the ASL[18]. Ok, now I knew what a CUP was, I thought I could do that without too much trouble. I didn't have to though, because I got really lucky and bumped into Conncetta1 who immediately offered to phone the ASL for me. Not only did she get the blood tests booked, she also rearranged the ECG for the same day. It was still going to be a shit week but was looking a lot less shit than it had been. All I had to do was cancel the duplicated scan.

In the afternoon, I got a phone call from Chieti hospital

---

[18] Local administrative centre for public health.

with an appointment for Radiotherapy. I typed a new schedule for the side of the fridge. Having things typed up made me feel less out of control.

Later on, Cristina called again to say that the Mayor had made sure we were at top of the COVID vaccination list. We would hopefully be jabbed the following Saturday. She would drop off the documents that I needed to fill in.

Meantime the post lady arrived with a parcel for me. It was from my sister. Inside was an amazing jumper hand-knitted by one of her old ladies. I loved it, especially being so unexpected.

April 8th

Back in Ortona for a bone scan, I first went to the CUP to cancel the (same) bone scan appointment I had erroneously booked in Chieti. for the 15th. This time, I had prepared and rehearsed what I need to say so it was remarkably easy. Had they asked me any questions it might have been a different story. There is only so much you can prepare in advance.

With the extra scan cancelled I needed to find where to get this scan done. The notice board wasn't any help but there was a guard in uniform manning a desk in the central hall, so I asked him. He said 'no problem - hang on and I'll show you' which I thought was exceptionally nice of him. It was just a few seconds wait. Just long enough for him to finish rolling his cigarette and put his tobacco away. Be fair, He wasn't actually smoking in the reception of the cancer hospital; just preparing his ciggies for later consumption.

The guard took me to the room with the scanning machine. This particular scan - MOC-DEXA radiche lombare & femore – was apparently for measuring bone density and, remembering the MRI (do not be afraid!) I was more than a bit apprehensive about it. I didn't have to worry. On the scale of Big Scary Machines it only registered as a 3 or 4. You simply lie flat while a curved machine passes over your body very closely and that's it. They gave me my results pretty much straight away.

April 9th

I finally and literally reached the stage where I could turn over in bed and not have to sleep flat on my back. I could do a whole 10 minutes.

April 10th

Saturday should have been a day off except it was Covid vaccination day. The vaccinations were being given at a sports centre about 20 minutes away, so Cristina called for me and we drove there together. People had been booked in groups, with each group waiting in the car park until it was called. Socially distanced of course. Once called, we walked down a steep slope to stand in a second socially distanced queue. The only people under the age of 80 in the queue were their carers ... and us. We stood out like a sore thumb. I wanted a badge that said 'I'm not pushing in honest, I know I look healthy but I've got cancer, honestly I have. I can show you my scar if you like,' That's quite a lot of text to get on just one badge though. It's probably even more in Italian.

We had to go in separately so, following Cristina and watching what she did, I handed over my sheaf of papers to a woman sitting at the entry desk. After she had counter-signed them I took them through to a second desk where I answered a few (fortunately easy) questions. At the third desk I was given a bar code. Just three desks and two lots of signatures was pretty good going.

I won't describe the vaccination process because by now we've all had them (or I hope you have) and I can't imagine it's very different country to country.

April 11th

You remember I no longer had to sleep flat on my back? I was thrilled when that happened. I was, therefore, less than thrilled to turn over and be woken up by pain again. Not the pain in my breast; the pain in my arm. Bloody vaccination!!

12 A BUSY BODY

Becoming a human reactor, Prince Phillip dies, another Big Scary Machine appears, testing goes wild and medicine integrata calls.

April 12th

The week began with a Scintigrafia Ossea Whole Body. That's what it was called. So why are the first two words in Italian and the last two in English? I don't know either. I also had no real idea what it was, but I was about to find out. It was in the same place where I had the radioactive thing before so I suspected that radioactive stuff would be involved again.

On my way in a man stopped me in the hospital corridor. I thought he wanted to ask me directions to somewhere (and I was already thinking fat chance) but he just wanted to tell me I had beautiful eyes. As good starts to the week go, that had to be one of my best ever.

By 9.30am, third in the queue, I was already checked in. Just like before, there were forms to sign, birth dates to check, explanations to be made and plastic overshoes to wear. Just like before, I went through to the inner waiting toom and then into what I called the injection room.

The doctor, preparing another fearsome looking steel needle, asked me what I thought about Prince Phillip (who had just died). Looking at the needle I chose my words carefully and tactfully. He injected me and the nurse parked me back in the first waiting room. I was told I would have little radioactive jobbies coursing through my body for the next 2 days and shouldn't go near any small children.

I watched TV which was full of the news about Prince Philip. Trying to translate soon became boring so I opened my kindle to read instead. As I read, the nurse took another woman into and back out of the injection room. The nurse looked around the room and then at me. "You". She beckoned me back inside and I was pleasantly surprised. I'd thought the wait would be longer.

It was. The reason she'd called me in was because the waiting room was too full (Covid) so would I mind staying in the injection room while I waited. Of course I didn't. Who wouldn't want to swap a hard upright plastic chair for a padded reclining couch.

"That's okay" I said blithely and added "How long for?".

"Oh about 2 hours."

Eek! As soon as she left I tried to call himself. He was waiting in the car park and would be furious if he sat there all morning with no word (as I would be). That was when I discovered the room was sealed in some way – presumably because of radiation - and I couldn't get a phone signal. WhatsApp wouldn't work either, nor would sending a normal message text. I tried standing by the door and I tried standing by the far wall, with no idea if it was an outside wall or not. I even tried standing on the chair and waving the phone at the ceiling. I kept pressing send message over and over hoping for a momentary break in the barrier. I don't know how or why but it finally worked, and I let him know I wouldn't be out until after lunch.

-0-

The actual bone scan when it arrived was immensely claustrophobic. I really did not like being strapped in place with a massive metal plate overhead about an inch away. I have no idea how long it took because I kept my eyes shut the whole time and tried to focus on my breathing rather than what happening. On the Big Scary Machine scale it only scored a 6 for big but it merited a good 9 for scary.

I was sent to the waiting room one last time while they prepared the report and then I was out of there. I read the report as I was walking out of the hospital and translated it in the car going home. So far as I could see I had some dodgy bone action going on in the cervical area- whether that meant near the neck or the womb I couldn't say.

I almost inhaled my lunch I was so bloody hungry by the time we get home.

April 13th

Casoli hospital – my third hospital so far – is only twenty minutes from home and I arrived early. At the entrance I was zapped for my temperature and signed pieces of paper to swear I had no Covid symptoms before going to the CUP / reception desk to hand in my ricetta. I should have known better but I was once again feeling pretty smug about myself. I knew the procedures by now and anyway, this was only a small hospital.

Well, guess what?

They couldn't find my blood test booking. The ECG booking was fine but there was no trace of the blood test booking on the computer. All my faux confidence vanished instantly. It took 30 minutes to sort it out. By the end, I had a headache from concentrating and a mild case of panic in my stomach.

When I eventually got the right bits of paper I followed directions to the blood testing area and was seen immediately. As the nurse drew my blood she asked me what I thought about Prince Phillip dying. I'd been asked this so many times by now I could reply easily and with fluency. This restored my confidence enough for me to remember Cristina's instructions to ask for my results online. Things were storming again.

-0-

With a long break before the ECG I left the hospital and went in search of a cornetto or something to eat. When I came back I looked on the signs to see where I should go. I located the floor easily enough but then drew a blank. I could

142

see nothing telling me where to go. Worse, because the hospital is mainly unused, I could see few places to ask. Well, none actually.

It was okay, I told myself. I was still early. I had lots of time to look.

I finally saw a piece of paper taped to a closed corridor door which suggested I was in the right place so I hung around for a bit in the deserted waiting room. This particular room – actually more of an area than a room, being a central hall with several corridors leading off - was one up on most that I had been in. It didn't just have a crucifix; it had a massive Madonna statue in one corner.

I looked around – oh my god! (if you'll pardon the expression) there was a statue in every corner! I was surrounded my images of the Virgin Mary. That was a bit alarming. How much trouble did you have to be in to need four Marys? How much trouble was I in? I was of course, thinking of chemotherapy again. It was never far from my mind at that stage.

My appointment was now in less than 10 minutes, and I still hadn't seen a soul. Maybe I was in the wrong place. It's not like it would have been my first mistake. I left the Madonnas and went to examine the door with the paper notice. I subtly tried the handle but it had one of those proper locks and pass key things on it so it wouldn't budge. I hovered outside hopefully and then, when a medical person eventually and finally emerged, I leapt on them.

Yes, they told me. I was in the right place. Yes, they would call me. I could relax.

-0-

The ECG when it happened was in a consulting room which seemed too large for its purpose. The one thing this little hospital wasn't short of was spare space. The nurse hooked me up and the doctor chatted to me about Prince Philip dying. We all agreed that the Queen was probably very upset.

The printed out my results and I was done. Time for an early lunch.

-0-

After a quick lunch we drove 45 minutes to Chieti hospital, this time for an ultrasound of my abdominal area. This was where my day began to go downhill.

I knew where the CUP was, so I was not worried about that. Instead, I went to Radiography, looking for where the ultrasound would be. It was not where I thought. I went back to the main reception and asked. The location they gave me was the same as the one I had written down. I tried again. It still wasn't where I thought. Nor was it in the next corridor. Or the next. I picked another reception desk at random and asked for actual directions this time. Then I followed what I thought they had told me.

I ended up in an abnormally long corridor opposite the CUP, panicked, came back, and found someone else to ask. They told me the same thing, so I retraced my steps and tried again. Starting from the CUP – deserted because it was still lunchtime by Italian reckoning, I followed the corridor opposite for an unfeasibly long distance, and far longer than felt comfortable. I was by now, moving at a fast trot. Suddenly, at last, the waiting room for the ultrasound clinic was in front of me. I checked the time. I was still early. No need to panic, but trotting was still called for.

I went back to the CUP to exchange my ricetta for the authorisation. Deserted twenty minutes ago it was now heaving. I got my ticket (a green number) from the machine and stood watching the display. At the beginning all of the numbers moved quite quickly and I relaxed; I would make it in time. But then there was a glut of blue numbers. And more blue numbers. And now a glut of red numbers. And more blue numbers again. And now the orange numbers were bidding for board supremacy. The green numbers had vanished. I was by now sweating and hopping from foot to foot. My appointment time was getting close. Should I run down the exceptionally long corridor and explain or would I miss my turn? The ticket numbers were so erratic I couldn't tell, and I decided not to risk it.

Finally, roughly three minutes after my appointed time, my number was called. I sprinted to the booth, threw my card and the ricetta through the gap and joggled from foot to foot, explaining I was late. As soon as I got the paper I needed, I turned and ran the entire length of the corridor like it as an Olympic sprint. Except you don't see many athletes holding onto their right breast to minimise the joggling. Or finishing as out of breath as I was.

It was okay, there was still someone (a nun) waiting in front of me. Actually, she wasn't waiting to be seen, just for her fellow nun to come out but I didn't know that, so I thought I was okay.

145

-0-

I sat down, panting. In just a few seconds, the door opened and a nurse and a nun came out. The nurse told the nun to wait and asked me my name. I handed over my sheet of paper and said I was sorry for being late. She looked from the paper to me.

"You're not Italian" she said accusingly

"No" I confessed, like it wasn't obvious. She sighed.

"It's okay" I reassured her. "I'll understand what you say, you just have to speak slowly."

She sighed again. More deeply. She could probably tell I was lying. She told me to wait.

After 15 minutes or so another nurse came out with a report for the waiting nun(s) and told me I could go through. She waved me through to a cubicle where the first nurse was waiting. "Strip off your top clothes and lie down" she told me in Italian, adding "HAI CAPITO?" very loudly. Then, in fractured English "Have you understand?" "Yes" I say, "I understood". I think she wouldn't have believed me, except I did as I'd been told.

While we were waiting for a doctor she set the machine up and squirted cold goo onto me. The deafening silence was uncomfortable so I said again, "You know it's okay, you can speak Italian to me". She looked at me with narrowed eyes but decided to give it a go.

"It's very sad about Prince Phillip" she said.

"Yes" I agreed. "It's very sad".

"Your queen must be very upset."

"Yes I think she is".

I wondered whether she'd forgive me for not being Italian if I told her I'd met both of them. She might just think it was another lie. I was still weighing up the pros and cons of name dropping when a (very) young doctor arrived. Unlike the nurse he was delighted I was English because, as he explained to me, he needed to practise his English.

Unfortunately, he was right – he really did need to practise and frankly it would have been a lot easier for both of us if he had spoken in Italian. I have a vision of the nurse going back into the staff area and saying 'would you believe it? as if my day couldn't get any worse we've got an English person out there now', and him jumping up saying 'Me, I'll do it, please let me do it'. However, it happened, I'm pretty certain that him turning up in my cubicle was no accident.

He slid the thingy that looks like a bit like a really fat electric razor without the razor bit (apparently, it's called a transducer) over each area, making me hold my breath every time he pressed into section. Sometimes twice. The breath holding was actually quite hard because it's for a long time; each time I was on the verge of exploding by the time to said to breathe again. Then he did each area again, and then a third time. By the third time I knew the routine and only needed the lightest finger pressure to move into position. But I was wondering why he kept going over the same area and why they were studying the display so intently. Something, I thought, must be wrong.

Bear in mind that it was only few weeks post operation and I was probably overdue for a wave of self-pity. It arrived. In fact, it was a tsunami of self-pity There I was, lying on my side, completely on my own not knowing what was going on, staring at the same small patch of yellow wall for more than half an hour and I'd had enough. My nose prickled and my eyes filled with tears, and it was all I could do not to start howling out loud.

They turned me onto my back, and I surreptitiously wiped away the trail of saline that slid over the side of my face. The nurse went away and came back with a senior doctor who checked me over again. He lingered in exactly the same places, pressing the transducer down so hard that it hurt. Eventually, and for the first time, he looked at me.

"Did you eat lunch?" he asked.

"Yes…" I replied.

"You weren't supposed to".

"Well nobody told me that.." I started to say but he had already turned away and was telling the young doctor. "It's just lunch. She hasn't digested. You should had checked. It's nothing to worry about.

He turned back to me. "It's nothing to worry about" he repeated. "It's just fat".

Oh great, now I was fat as well. To be fair, I don't know if he was talking about me or my liver, it could easily have been either.

148

Like the nun before me, I waited outside for my results and, as soon as I had them, started the long corridor trek back to the CUP. I was almost at the end when I heard my name being called and turned. The nurse was running after me with my medical file. I'd left it in the cubicle. I think it was the shock of being called fat that made me forget it.

That evening one of the cats was chased up a tree and managed to strand itself on my neighbour's roof.

April 14th

The next day I was back in Chieti hospital for a radiotherapy appointment. As I didn't have a bit of paper for this (just a verbal instruction by telephone) I strode confidently to radiography and announced myself at the check in desk. That's when they told me that radiotherapy wasn't in radiology and I needed to be somewhere else entirely. It was the two radios that misled me.

Radiotherapy was some distance away which meant I was late by the time I got there. I don't know why, but Chieti's radiotherapy department had the best waiting room I had yet been in. It actually had soft chairs in place of plastic ones, and flowers and magazines on the coffee tables. The reception area was a large, open plan office with glassed walls, and I could see several people, including someone who was clearly the receptionist, working at desks inside. All of whom completely ignored me standing in front of the check in window.

I had been standing, ignored, for about 5 increasingly desperate minutes when a woman in a white lab coat went into inside and deposited some papers into a filing cabinet. She looked at me through the glass and said something to the receptionist. I don't know what she said but the receptionist finally came over to ask me what I wanted. I said I had an appointment and gave her my Tessera Sanitaria which she took and handed to the white coated woman. There was a lot of discussion that I couldn't follow but this time it's because they were standing at the back of the office. For once it was because I actually couldn't hear anything, rather than not understanding anything.

The white coated woman came out and told me to follow her. Turned out she was the radiologist.

An hour later, it was clear that my lovely smiley surgeon had serious competition for my "Favourite Cancer Specialist of the Year Award'. Equally friendly and reassuring, this doctor's Italian was so beautifully clear that I easily followed 95% of what she said. Any words I didn't know she immediately typed into Google Translate to get the right English words for me. Well, mainly the right words. Anybody who uses Google Translate knows that it's not always that reliable; looking for English equivalence words is more than a bit sledgehammer-ish at times. But we enjoyed discussing where the words were wrong.

At first, everything went swimmingly. She explained how radiotherapy works. She told me why they were doing it (basically to completely sterilise the breast and zap any teensy-weensy cancer cells that might had made a run for it). She told me how long it would last (every weekday for up to 5 weeks) and what the likely side effects would be (more on that later). She gave me a booklet to take home and read. She told me all about her son who was currently working in Coventry.

Then it went downhill as she told me that she wouldn't actually be doing my radiotherapy. It seemed the reason I had been referred to Teramo for treatment was because Chieti had a 6-month waiting list. "Obviously" she said, "that list can fluctuate as peoples' need for treatment might change" (like they've died I thought), "but even if it does come down it does not help you. Ideally, you ought to have the treatment in the next three months". Although, she added, I couldn't actually begin anything until they decided if I needed chemotherapy or not. If I did have to have chemotherapy, then the radiotherapy window would be extended and Chieti might become a possibility.

I was a bit devastated by this news. Much as I wanted to go to Chieti and this particular doctor, having chemotherapy didn't seem like a fair trade. Yet Teramo? That meant driving four or more hours each day. It wasn't really tenable. She agreed and said she'd refer me to Pescara to see if I could get in there instead. But even so, as I said to Himself in the car going home, Pescara is an hour and a quarter away and not ideal. Himself said we'd manage somehow. And if Pescara was full-up too, we'd hire an Airbnb and move to Teramo for a month.

When I got home I had a phone call from Pescara hospital confirming that a radiotherapy request had been made. I should wait to hear.

April 16th

For my second check-up at Chieti I knew where I was going and I knew the routine. I was all ready. Back in the room with Senior and Junior, I handed over all my test results and sat waiting while they went through them. I felt like I was having

151

an exam marked.

I passed.

Everything was good.

What was more, they had my results back from the lab and the news couldn't have been better. I didn't have to have chemotherapy.

I was given what was practically a booklet with my lab results to keep. The diagrams and explanations were clear, even being in Italian, with lots of lovely graphs and big numbers. Bottom line it said my score was ER 9.6, PR 7.4; that with medication the chance of recurrence after 9 years was down to 7%; and that having chemotherapy would offer me a less than 1% benefit. Diddly squat in other words.

I would have to have a check-up in November and at intervals after that, but basically I was good.

Senior left the room to organise my next appointment date and authorise my medications, leaving me with Junior. In both sessions, Junior had deferred to Senior and not yet said not a single word directly to me but that was about to change.

She sprang to life as soon as the door closed behind Senior. "Where was I from? What was I doing I Italy? What made me decide to move?" She told me she had been to London twice. Once with her parents which was really boring and once with her friends which was totally brilliant. She asked me for a good place to stay in London if she went again. She told me she wanted to go again the next year, Covid willing. She confided that she'd learned some English at school, but she'd forgotten it all now. She wanted to know what I had done to learn Italian and how long I'd been studying.

The massive torrent of words ceased the second the door reopened to admit Senior, with the date of my next appointment. She also had a list of tests I would have to arrange the week before I come back for my 6-month check. More scans and blood tests basically. Before I left, she made me two prescriptions. One was for Letrozole and the other for D-Base (a supplement to keep my bones healthy). The final thing she said was congratulations, I could go.

April 17th

Pescara hospital called. I had an appointment for the following Friday. The list of instructions I was given was long and complicated with specific mention of not doing something with something yellow which was below something else. I know. When I put my phone down and looked at what I'd written I couldn't make any sense of it either.

I went to the Farmacia to collect the tablets I had been prescribed. They were not held in stock, so I had to go back for them that same evening. This was what would happen almost every time from now on.

April 23rd

Despite Pescara being a 45-minute drive, an hour max, we left home at 10am for the appointment at noon. This time (unusually) it was me insisting on leaving early because I didn't know the hospital and I was scared of traffic problems.

We almost needed it all. By the time we had negotiated

the traffic and found a parking space it had taken us almost 90 minutes to get to Pescara hospital. No way, I thought, was this going to be feasible every day for four or five weeks.

Inside, past the electronic temperature check, the department was clearly signposted for once. It was simply down one flight of stairs, turn right and along the corridor. Even I couldn't get lost.

The door to the department was at the end of the corridor and couldn't be entered without permission - you had to be buzzed through by the receptionist. When I reached the door and saw the entry phone I realised what the telephone call was about. There were two buttons you could press- the top one for reception and lower one (a yellow button) for radiotherapy itself. Of course, I couldn't remember if they said to press the yellow button or definitely not to press the yellow button so, exactly 5 minutes before my appointment, I hedged my bets and pressed both at once. Judging by the expression on the receptionist's face I don't think that was the right thing to do.

Inside I had to hand over my entire file and ID documents, complete a Covid questionnaire, sign more forms and then wait for 40 minutes. The actual appointment was very quick. It was the same process as Chieti (forms, brief look at my breast, questions) but missing the after-care advice because the previous doctor had given me this already. Really it was just a matter of this doctor signing me into the programme and getting my signature on documents. I liked her, but that might be because she actually smiled at my 'no, well apart from cancer joke' when I was asked about existing illnesses.

I was given my next appointment. It was for the May 11th, about two and a half weeks away so, with a few weeks clear of any more tests and appointments it was time to think about visiting Medicine Integrata.

I wrote an email to Medicine Integrata saying I was interested in coming along. I explained that I was English just in case they thought this was a barrier in any way – most of the programme seemed to be advice based so they might think it would be too difficult to communicate.

-0-

Cara rang. People are refusing to have the Astra Zeneca vaccine (holding out for Pfizer) so if Himself is happy to take Astra Zeneca he can sign up now. He wasn't happy. He was ecstatic.

April 24th

The phone rang and it was a man from Medicine Integrata. We had a bit of a chat, switching from Italian to English and back again (his English was quite good so we managed well between us) and he was quite happy that the programme would benefit me. The only thing was, I couldn't go until after the radiotherapy. I told him I thought that would be happening in June. Before we finished, I asked him if it would be okay to do yoga and he said that doing yoga breathing exercises was a really good idea. Hmmm. I was really thinking of actual yoga.

April 26th

I received an email with my Medicine Integrata appointments. They are set for the 6th and 15th July and I will need more tests before I go. They've sent me a list.

April 27th

Thinking I might need this information when I go to the Medicine Integrata appointment I made a note of what had been happening to me post operation, and especially now that I was taking Letrozole.

First, the pain. Thanks to the magical OKI powders it had never been too bad. The site of the pain shifted often. In the beginning it was most frequently in my breast itself, then my armpit joined in, and now I was getting the occasional pain in the back of my shoulder. For quite a long period I had no sensation of touch on the back of my shoulder at all. You could easily have poked a needle in me and I wouldn't have known. By now though, it felt more numb than completely dead, but with the added bonus of pain twinges that I knew would get worse as it healed more.

The side of my breast was numb too. I could feel a lump along the line of scar tissue but it was reducing and visually it looked great, insofar as a scar that goes across your breast can. The scar line was very neat and contoured to the breast so it didn't scream at you - I could easily visualise a time when it would be hardly noticeable.

Next, movement. It was still limited but with exercise was getting better daily. The pain when reaching up and over my head was gone – by now I just felt a slight tug. The only stretch that was making me pause (stop dead in my tracks) was reaching forwards and upwards at the same time. Think of taking something from a high shelf and you'll get the idea. I thought that might tie into the numbness on my shoulder blades and resolved to start yoga again.

Sleeping was hard. I was tired all the time but with no exercise my body was awake. I found I could sleep for a maximum of 90 minutes before I woke up - normally dripping with sweat too. For some reason, after the second time I woke up, it would take more than an hour to go back to sleep.

Two other things happened that I really didn't expect. One was that my skin (all over) was very dry. The other was joint or bone pain: I had an occasional pain in one or other of my femurs when waking and an ache in my knees. I had never had anything like this before and couldn't see any reason why it should be happening, but it was.

May 2nd

Second Covid Vaccination

May 3rd

I woke up feeling rough and by 5pm was laying on the settee wrapped in blankets. I fall asleep for two hours, woke up, and went to the bathroom to vomit. All my joints hurt. I was shivery. I gave up and went to bed at 10 o'clock. As an afterthought I took some Ibufopren ... and felt fine within half an hour. I can't believe it didn't occur to me to take something earlier.

13 RADIOTHERAPY PART ONE

A Big Scary Machine with disconcertingly pretty lights, dashed expectations on timing, the kindness of strangers, new aches and pains arrive, the famous magic cream, more horrible bras and twinges take over from numbness.

May 11th

My first radiotherapy appointment was to be a test run. This information would normally have disappointed me, but my three breast cancer buddies each told me that this was to be expected. That's three buddies who have been through breast cancer by the way, not three friends in total. That would be sad.

I was feeling sick. Just a few weeks without any appointments had stripped away my already thin veneer of confidence and this alternate reality felt too strange to be real all over again. Worse, the people coming out as I was about to go in all looked alarmingly sick to me. I was early anyway so I stood in the corridor deep breathing, 6 counts in, 10 counts out. I was putting off pressing the bell and having to talk to a high velocity receptionist who may or may not be impatient with me.

-0-

The receptionist was lovely. As soon as I had disinfected my hands and completed the obligatory Covid contact form she came out from the office and walked me through the process, showing me exactly where to go. I tried to memorise the instructions she gave me for future visits. They were to:

Press the entry phone for reception NOT radiotherapy.

Disinfect your hands when you come in.

Pass your Tessera Sanitaria over the card reader (on the reception ledge) and take the ticket it gives you. This will be your appointment number.

Take your ticket and advance to the next set of sealed doors. Pass your Tessera Sanitaria over the card reader on the wall to open the doors.

Go into the waiting room immediately on the right. When it is your turn, the number you have taken will appear on the screen and you should go straight to the treatment room.

It was all deliciously clear, and I thanked her profusely.

Two people were in the waiting room, sitting on opposite sides of the room. I took a chair against the third wall, and we said hello but nothing else. After a while they were both called through leaving me alone. That was when I realised that I had absolutely no idea where the treatment rooms were. Bugger.

I watched the screen but nothing was moving. I read all the extra bits on the screen about how to exit after therapy and how it was strictly forbidden to queue jump or pick up someone else's number.

When I ran out of things to read on the screen I got up and read the notice board by the entrance. I was thinking that if I hovered there long enough, somebody who looked like they might know something might walk by. They didn't, but I did read a great notice. It said

"si ricorda che la terapia vengono eseguite secondo l'orario assegnato"

Translated this reads

"we remind you that the therapy will be carried out according to the assigned schedule".

Except that someone has handwritten 'non' before the word 'vengono', so it actually says

"we remind you that the therapy is not carried out according to the assigned schedule".

I liked that a frustrated someone has scribbled on their notice. I liked it even more that they'd left it there.

I heard a bing sound and looked at the screen. My number was there, and I had to go to treatment room X (It wasn't room X but I can't remember what it was called now).

I didn't know where room X was. I went into the corridor but there were no clues there. I could feel panic rising up but then a head appeared round an entranceway accompanied by a voice that said Senora Stratton? "Si" I replied. "Vieni" she said, and the head disappeared.

Through the entranceway was another corridor area, but not empty. This one was lined with desks, computers and monitors with people (maybe 5 in total) all looking at the monitors, making notes and generally being busy. They all looked up and smiled at me. Buon Giorno we all said in turn.

A door on the left opened and a man appeared.

"Senora Stratton?"

"Si."

"Prego…viene".

I went into a large room dominated by a large machine. On the Big Scary Machine (BSM) scale it rated a 6. Either that or I was getting blasé. This one was a flat table with what looked like a circular doughnut around it. I thought (I was right) that the table probably passed your prone body through the doughnut.

He showed me to a changing cubicle at the back of the room and told me to take my top clothes off. When I came back I lay down on the table. "Ooh nice job" he said, looking at my breast. And then "pretty eyes" looking at my apprehensive orbs above my mask. I do love Italian men.

I lifted my arms to hold onto a bar above my head and he shifted me until he was satisfied. I could see a dolphin painted into the ceiling. They must have moved the machine because it wasn't directly overhead. Squinting down my body I could see red beams of light criss-crossing it and then the table moved so that my upper torso was inside the doughnut ring. Here, the machine slid two points down the Big Scary scale, because I could now see pretty red lights all around the circle of the doughnut. Even better, they went all whizzy whizz and then span really fast like the spin cycle on a washing machine.

When all this was done and I was ejected from the doughnut he tattooed four small black dots on me. One under each arm, one in the centre of my breasts and the other a few inches below. The tattooing was actually quite painful when he wiggled the dye in, but it was only momentary. He asked if I was allergic to plasters then covered the tattooed parts up. The plasters didn't stop the dye leaking all over my bra, but as it was one of the horrible old lady cotton bras I really didn't care.

Just as he was finishing another, older man came in. He wandered over and looked at my breast. "Ooh nice job" he said. "Who did it for you? Were you at Ortona?" We had a chat about my experience so far and he said he was sorry that the level of service had dropped so badly today. "He's new" he said, indicating the tattooing technician. "I hope he didn't make too much of a mess of it. Don't be too worried though, he's not the worst that we have". It was all very jovial and obviously a well-worn routine.

Just as I was getting off the table I made the mistake of asking how long it would be before my treatment proper started. I can't tell you what he said in detail because I clearly hit a nerve and lost track after about the third sentence. Suffice to said that resources were involved, and waiting lists and then I think we might have moved onto everything else that was wrong with the world. All I could think of was the fact that I was standing there, quite literally half naked, in front of a total stranger. I really, really wanted to go and put my clothes back on. I didn't interrupt though. Like an idiot I just stood there nodding and smiling and oohing and pretending to understand. I actually didn't have a clue what he was saying to me. All I did manage to grasp was that he couldn't tell me when it would be, but it would be AT LEAST (his emphasis) a few weeks.

-0-

When I emerged, safely dressed, they asked me to take my mask off and took a photograph. For the first time in this process, it was my face that was photographed, not my breast. As I emerged into the corridor everyone said goodbye and see you soon. I liked that.

Not knowing when the treatment might be, Himself and I agreed to take the risk of booking an Airbnb for me, starting in two weeks. After all, at least two weeks might mean actually two weeks, and with Pescara being a holiday town, things would be getting booked up. Pescara in summer is always heaving with visitors.

May 25th

I was in Pescara with himself. Not for radiotherapy – that hoped for date had been and gone – but for a long weekend by the sea. Having paid for an Airbnb we thought we might as well use it, but now we were about to go home again. I was leaving all my clothes in the apartment we had rented as we still had three and a half weeks rental left. Not to mention I may have had to come back at a moment's notice.

Back home I asked Cristina if she would call Pescara Hospital for me. Maybe she could get a date from them. She pointed out – quite rightly - that I could easily have gone there and asked while I was in Pescara but, being a darling she did it anyway. She came back with mid-June as a possible start date. The word 'possible' was heavily stressed. I had to wait until they called me. Basically, it was a don't call us, we'll call you situation. Which is equally demoralising in any language.

Cristina also discovered that the initial doctor had missed out one of the letters of my surname, which meant I was registered wrongly. She told me I needed to email them a copy of my "documento di identità."

May 29th

We were back in Pescara for the weekend and about to meet up with Leo, the owner of the Airbnb. He had a second flat next door which was used as a sometime office and sometime Airbnb so he'd noticed that we'd gone and called us, concerned to know why. Himself explained the situation, Leo said he would like to discuss it, so here we were.

When Leo arrived he had a solution. He said we should cancel the Airbnb and get a refund for the remaining time. We said that wasn't fair to him. He shrugged. He just thought it was the right thing to do. Would you be able to re-let it? We asked. He said no, it was too short notice so we reiterated that it wasn't fair on him. Besides, I could be called at any moment so we might well need it. In the meantime we could use it at weekends and enjoy Pescara. Eventually we compromised. We wouldn't cancel and he wouldn't refund us, but if we wanted an Airbnb in the future he would give us 5 days free.

He called it a compromise. We called it incredibly generous. Once again, I was stunned by the kindness of strangers.

May 31st

I was already bored of taking a tablet every morning and ready to imagine any side effects.

This morning I had woken up and tried to decide what bits of me hurt the most. It was a competition between the pain in my left hip and the ache in my right knee and I was so fed up of it. Overnight it seemed - or at least since recovering from the operation and starting medication - I'd gone from just waking up to waking up with some sort of pain in place. It wasn't a really bad pain, more of an irritating ache, but it was predictable and it was there and it was never there before. Plus I was exhausted because I was laying awake half the night, either because of a hot flash or because Himself was snoring.

This time when I woke up in the middle of the night (snoring provoked) I began to worry about the radiotherapy and when exactly it was going to start. It didn't help that Himself was asking me every day if I've had a phone call yet. Sometimes I just wanted to yell at him "yes they called me last week but I've been keeping it secret from you!". I didn't because I know he was as worried as I was.

June 2nd

With copious advice from my three breast cancer buddies I had been shopping to buy cream, ready for the radiotherapy. On the advice of one I bought pure aloe vera. On the advice of another I bought aqueous cream. On the advice of my pharmacist I bought the cream he recommended for post radiotherapy. They all disagreed on what the best cream was to buy was, but they all agreed that cream was an absolute lifesaver. To quote one I 'would live for the moment I applied it'. This was at the same time they were all telling me that radiotherapy 'was a breeze' and I would 'sail though it'. Mixed messages or what?

I also bought some alarmingly expensive shower gel that said it contained nothing harmful in any way. It turned out to be so good, and so frugal to use that I planned to keep buying it. Sorry Dove.

Finally, and reluctantly, I went onto the Amazon site and ordered another of the old lady white cotton bars, except this one was black. I knew I'd have to go back into the monstrosities while I had radiotherapy and the Italian summer was almost upon us. Two bras were never not going to hack it unless I washed and dried one every night. I sulked about this for days.

June 8th

By now, having heard nothing, I was getting a bit antsy. Nowhere near as antsy as Himself was but nonetheless antsy. Apart from anything else we were coming up to the magic three months window for treatment that the first radiotherapy consultant had mentioned. This time I wrote to Cara and asked if she or Thumper (my actual registered doctor) would call and chase it up for me.

Cara replied to me a few hours later with a partial success to report. They hadn't managed to get an actual start date, but it was as near as dammit. I would be called during the week from the 21st to the 25th of June. They had also confirmed that I shouldn't worry about the 3 months deadline because it was just approximate and I was perfectly on time

166

June 16th

Time for another progress check. Things were good. I had sensation back in my shoulder – it had gone from numb to being painful to the touch as the nerve endings grew back. In fact, there was one week when, all of a sudden, the side of my breast and under my arm became impossibly, painfully sensitive. It was so bad that I couldn't wear even the too big old lady cotton bra. That pain lasted about 8 days then vanished overnight. Now I had the odd sudden sharp twinge in my breast and that was about it.

The movement in my arm and shoulders was vastly improved. I still had to remember not to carry anything heavy or do something like twisting and lifting at the same time (ouch), but the point was I had to remember to remember. That was real progress.

June 22nd

The phone call arrived. My first radiotherapy appointment would be at noon the following day.

14 RADIOTHERAPY: THE FIRST HALF

The importance of air conditioning, an even Bigger Scarier Machine, my very own magic cream, a breakthrough with the reluctant pharmacist, the most eccentric Airbnb in Italy, the significance of sweat, more new bras, an Airbnb that's also an office and Italy win a football match.

June 23rd - June 25th (Therapy days 1 – 3)

The weather was now really hot, making the drive to Pescara seem longer than it actually is.

I arrived for my first appointment half an hour early (no surprise there) and took advantage of someone's exit to go straight into reception. Whereupon I was told to go straight back outside and wait in the corridor.

Two minutes before my appointment time a man came out to collect me. He told me I was late. I said I wasn't, that I'd been there half an hour. Well that wasn't right either according to him. He said that I should be arriving 15 minutes before my appointment, no more and no less. I wanted to dislike him because I don't like being told off, but he then ran all through the admission procedures with me again. It was apparent that I'd completely forgotten everything I'd been told, so I instantly forgave him. He also told me which entrance I had to go through when I was called. (It was the same corridor as before but still, I appreciated the gesture).

-0-

When my ticket was called and I went through, a nurse was waiting to show me where the changing rooms were. There were two curtained cubicles, on the opposite (right hand side) of the corridor, obliquely opposite the treatment room I was in before. Last time all I noticed were the banks of computers and the one room I went into. This time I noticed that the corridor ended in a massive pair of sealed doors with radiation warning lights overhead. The doors were closed and the lights were flashing.

The nurse gestured me into the empty cubicle, gave me a gown and told me I was to take it with me when I was finished; it was mine for the duration. She said I should take all my top clothes off, put the gown on and wait to be called. I should bring my bag with me. I changed and waited, lurking at the entrance to the cubicle.

A tall, rather beautiful woman appeared, followed by the nurse. The woman, clutching a hospital gown together at her chest, smiled vaguely at me, said Buon Giono and disappeared into the other cubicle. The nurse looks at me. "Vieni" she said and I followed her.

The massive doors at the end of the corridor were now open, revealing a short, very wide corridor that curved around and out of sight. It was painted the most beautiful bright yellow. We went into this and emerged into a treatment room with one of the largest Big Scary Machines I had seen so far. There was the usual central bed but this machine had so many parts attached to it, it was impossible to guess what might happen once you were on it.

After I'd taken my gown and shoes off I had to lay on the table which was then raised up. I was told to lift my arms and hold onto a bar above my head and two people shifted me about a bit. I tried to help but I was told not to. The positioning seemed to be very precise. Numbers were mentioned and I was shifted again. When they were satisfied, they left the room reminding me not to move. This first session was a bit of a blur. I knew that the machine made a lot of clicking noises, whirred and moved and then moved back to the original position but that was all I remembered. Later, of course, I became very familiar with the routine. This time, when a voice over the loudspeaker told me I could lower my arms, I was surprised at how quick it had been. 5 minutes? 10 maximum.

While I was still on the table a doctor (technician?) came in to explain that I would have 20 sessions, Monday to Friday, at the same time each day. Right now I should get dressed and go back to the waiting room. Someone would talk to me.

-0-

Once collected from the waiting toom I was taken to a small office where a doctor – again – explained all the possible side effects of radiotherapy. "If you experience anything untoward" she said "You must say at once. And here is a cream (aha! the magic cream!) that you must use. This cream is for you to take but here also is a prescription that you must get from the farmacia. You must apply it morning and evening, as far away from the treatment as possible. Now you can go." I did. It was just one o'clock. It was both the longest and the shortest hour of my life.

-0-

At home I took my prescription to the pharmacist in my commune but they didn't have the magic cream in stock. Tomorrow being their closed day it would be Friday before I could get it, so I decided to try the farmacia in the next commune along. I was not sure how far the sample would go.

Most times when I go into the farmacia in the next commune there are two women serving, one older and one younger who normally serves me. This time when I went in, the younger women wasn't there.

The older pharmacist looked at me in horror. It was a look I knew well. It said 'Oh no! no! no! no! no! no! no! no! That English woman's coming in and there's nobody else here to speak to her. I won't be able to understand her! She won't be able to understand me! This is a nightmare!'. I used to get that look a lot. I still do, although less and less these days. At that time though, this particular woman was still terrified of me coming in.

I smiled reassuringly (I hoped) and gave her the prescription. It was not actually a prescription as such because I had to pay for it, but it was something official, with the hospital's name and the doctor's signature on it. She took it, looked at it, looked back at me, looked at it again and hesitated. Then…

"Cancro?" she ventured.

"Si" I replied. "Di seno". I waved vaguely at my right breast. "My radiotherapy started today".

"You had an operation?"

"Yes. A mastectomy[19] and reconstruction".

"Where? Ortona?"

"Yes"

"When?"

"March"

"Mine was last year" she said.

And that was it. All thoughts of it being too difficult to try and talk to the English woman were forgotten. We were sisters in breast cancer and that transcended all barriers.

She told me that I must talk about my cancer and that it was not something to be ashamed of. I found this fascinating, I'd thought of being devastated and angry, but it had never occurred to me to be ashamed. We should be open about these things she said, and I told her that I was being – well apart from not telling my mother. We discussed why my mother hadn't been told and she agreed that that was okay.

When the younger woman came back, I was not passed

---

[19] I understand that it was more accurately a partial mastectomy in that they didn't take the entire breast, but this was easier to say in Italian than the proper words. It still is.

over to her as I usually was (like a hot potato). Instead "the English has breast cancer like me" the older lady said, and now we were a conversation of three.

"Did you go to Ortona too?"

"Yes"

"Who did you have?"

I ashamedly admitted that I didn't know names but they readily accepted how much of a blur it had all been, not helped by the language issue.

"But everyone at Ortona is good. You were very lucky to go there".

I said I agreed. More than that, I told them how lucky I felt to be in Italy because the health service had been brilliant. They pulled a few faces at this – it's not the Italian way to be too effusive about anything to do with the state – but it was nice that I thought so. When I quit the shop, with my big jar of magic cream in hand and almost 20 euros poorer, I had made two new friends and I was happy.

-0-

We went out to eat that night. It was still blazingly hot and I was sweating. Specifically, I was sweating under the band of my bra. I surreptitiously wiped a hand under my breast and yikes!! It was like a nuclear thermo reactor (I am of course assuming that a nuclear thermo reactor is hot. I've really no idea if it is or not, but if it is I can promise you it isn't quite as hot as my titty was). Himself didn't want to but I insisted he felt my breast (in the middle of the street) so he could appreciate just what was going on there.

-0-

The rest of the First Week of Radiotherapy was only two days, so we drove in each day. It was tedious doing the journey each day but the appointment being in the middle of the day made it easier. I had booked an Airbnb for the following week and Leo had given us the free week he promised for the week after, so there was only the third week and a bit to sort out. I used the magic cream every morning and night and, so far, had had no side effects.

June 28th to July 2nd (Therapy days 4 – 8)

I was staying in the most amazingly eccentric Airbnb ever. The main room, painted in brilliant blue, red and yellow, had something to intrigue on every surface and wall. Hand-crafted wooden cabinets lining the kitchen walls contrasted with the cupboards made of old wineboxes. The fireplace was an art-deco marvel. A defunct entry-phone must have been one of the first examples ever manufactured. Lighting for the main room was looped through an ancient stepladder hanging parallel to the ceiling. In the corner, an empty champagne demijohn housed a glitter sprayed pom-pom. The bathroom boasted a floor to ceiling wine rack shuttered by stained glass doors. The tiny toilet was dominated by a beautiful marble, art nouveau mirror. There were clouds and swallows painted onto the bedroom ceiling and diamond cut-outs in the shutters. These were filled with coloured glass that made waking up feel magical.

Probably the best thing about it though, was that it used to be the cantina. It was thus blissfully cool, even without the air conditioning switched on. Did I mention that summer had arrived with a vengeance?

-0-

The hospital was an easy 11-minute walk door to door and I soon found a routine. By sheer good fortune I had been commissioned to do some work precisely when I had these empty hours to fill, so I worked until 11.30, then went to radiotherapy. After the therapy, if it wasn't too blazingly hot, I wandered into the city centre and had lunch at one of the bars before going back to work some more. In the early evening I explored the neighbourhood and bought something fresh to cook. It was lonely but not unbearable.

-0-

When I arrived at radiotherapy the first day my skin was damp. Thinking I had put the magic cream on too recently the nurse told me off. "You have been told" she said "to apply the cream as far away from your appointment as possible". I didn't tell her the truth – that it was actually sweat from walking in searing heat for 11 minutes. I'd rather be scolded.

Truth is, I'd sweated so much that my bra was soaking. You could have wrung it out with your bare hands. It was pretty disgusting trying to put it back on. That night I hand washed it and put a spare bra in my bag to change into after the next day's session. I added a small towel for last minute sweat wiping and then I had to scour the internet for yet more boring cotton bras to buy. I only had three and, at two bras a day, it wasn't going to be enough.

On my second night in the Airbnb I re-read the information I'd been given about radiotherapy and realised I was not supposed to be wearing anti perspirant. It was actually one of the big no-nos. Oops. But seriously? In that heat and without anti-perspirant I'd be stinking like a chinghiale inside 10 minutes. I solved it with a quick trip to the supermarket to buy baby wipes and a roll on anti-perspirant. From then on, inside the changing room I would remove my anti-perspirant with a baby wipe then reapply it as soon as I'd finished. I still don't know if this was breaking the rules or not but, just in case it was, I used a roll-on deodorant. That way I was less likely to leave a tell take perfume behind me.

-0-

Himself told me there was an amazon parcel waiting for me at home. It was new bras. Hours of research on the internet had finally located some non-underwired bras that seemed acceptable. I couldn't wait to get home and get rid of the horrible cotton jobs.

-0-

As the week went on and I became more accustomed to the Big Scary Machine I started to notice more of what was happening. I realised that I was not just laying on the bed, but that the neck rest had been pre-sized for me and placed so that I was always in the right position. I only know this because I was particularly nifty one day and got there while they were still doing the change over from the tall beautiful woman.

There was still always a bit of shifting (the number 95 was always mentioned) and they always refreshed the tattoo dot under my right arm. When I examined it I could see why.

Unlike the others its was barely visible.

This meant that all my horrible old lady bras soon had a small and indelible black mark on the band, where the felt tip had rubbed off of my skin. Not to put too fine a point on it, my skin was a little 'dewey' by the time I'd walked back to the Airbnb each day. The temperature was in the high 30s and even though I tried to hand wash both bras every day it wasn't enough to get the marks out. Did I care? No, not really. I hated those bras.

Sometimes they played music in the radiotherapy room. Sometimes they didn't. Some of the nurses chatted to me ('what are you doing today, where do you live?' that kind of thing) and others just issued instructions ('move up, hold on, stay still').

Anyway, back to the machine. As I lay there with my arms up, holding onto the bar, I could see the central part of the machine right above me. It was circular with a rectangular glass screen in its centre and had a piece of tape on it saying do not clean this machine or the glass. Behind the glass there were narrow black bars that began as a solid mass then separated to create an oddly shaped gap. The gap was always the same shape and after a few days I realised it was probably a profile of my breast. When the bars had finished opening the whole thing moved over to one side where I could no longer see it. I could hear a set piece of noises that culminated in a sustained beep; then it stopped, moved over my head again and to the other side where the sequence of noises were repeated.

When it returned to the centre for the second time and I saw the bars closing up again I knew it was finished, but I didn't move until I was told to, just in case.

There was no pain or even particularly any sensation. The hardest part was probably laying absolutely still for 5 minutes.

I lowered my arms when the staff came back in the room and told me I could. The bed would then be returned to it's starting height, low enough to dismount, and I could go. "Thank you" I would say. "See you tomorrow" they would say. And that was it.

-0-

On Friday I was packed and ready to go by 11 am. Himself arrived and drove me to the hospital which made me way too early, so I got chucked out into the corridor to wait. I saw a new sign saying that there would be no therapy the following Monday because they were doing maintenance on the machines, and when I checked with the technician, he confirmed that was right, That was a bit of a bugger because we had to be in Pescara on Sunday anyway. I would have liked an extra night at home.

Right now though, I had something else to look forward to. We'd already decided that we would go to a Japanese restaurant every Friday lunchtime as a 'reward for finishing the week'. I love Japanese food and it's a very rare treat where we live. We had a Bento box and yes, it was fantastic. Unfortunately it was also huge, and I discovered that actually, all I really wanted to do was to go home, so this was the only time we did it.

-0-

We were almost home when I remembered that all the dresses I'd taken with me and not worn were still in the wardrobe of the Airbnb. I didn't dare suggest we go back. Instead I phoned the owner and she agreed to keep them for me to pick up later.

At home I tried on the new bras that had arrived. Well, I tried one on. The band fit but the rest of it was like trying to cram watermelons into egg cups. The bras (all 6 of them) were a complete waste of money, especially as I didn't have the time or energy to organise a return. By this stage I'd spent more on bras in 4 months year than I had in the past 4 years and I still didn't have a single one that either fitted properly or looked half decent.

July 5th – 9th (therapy days 9 – 12)

We checked in at Leo's second Airbnb on the Sunday. This was the only day that suited him and as he was giving us a freebie it was the least we could do. This was the flat that doubled as an office and I thought it was perfect. There was a massive white board in the office/living room which I was allowed to use, a printer and a stack of office supplies. Working remotely had suddenly become a lot easier.

Other than the office, the flat had a reclining massage chair (bliss), effective portable air conditioners (more bliss) and a massive TV with an Amazon subscriptions which I thought would be bliss but ended up never watching. The one downside was the smallest kitchen I had ever seen in my life which made cooking nigh on impossible.

-0-

Monday being a day off I went back to last week's Airbnb to collect my dresses. Daniella, the Airbnb owner had put them, neatly folded, into a bag for me and invited me to take coffee and cake. I had long since learned that the polite (only possible) answer to this is always 'yes, thank you', so I did. We sat on her terrace, sheltered from the sun and I asked about all the weird and wonderful things she had in the rental.

I loved her explanation. Addicted to auctions and second-hand[20] shops, she can only justify her purchases by using them to decorate her rental apartments. She pulled me to the terrace edge and showed me the garden which was equally full of repurposed objects. There had been one particular object I had fallen in love with inside the apartment. It was so elegant, but I couldn't for the life of me work out what it was meant to be for, so I asked her. After I described it and where it was kept in the apartment she burst out laughing. She had no idea either.

-0-

I mentioned earlier about not sleeping well. That was still the case. Actually that's an understatement. I was hardly sleeping at all. On my own, I wasn't going to bed until after midnight and I was waking up every hour. Once a week, if I was lucky, I became so exhausted that I managed a full, proper 8 hours. So when it got to July 6th and I woke up with eyes that feel liked boiled eggs rolled in hot grit, I knew that I would be sleepi

ng well that night. I couldn't wait.

---

[20] Or 'vintage' if you prefer. It's all second-hand. Or third, or fourth. Eventually of course it becomes antique.

What I failed to factor in was the Football World Cup. The semi-final of the Football World Cup. Featuring Italy. Who won.

In bed by 11pm I was drifting nicely into sleep when the first car horns started. Followed by the whooping. And then the singing. At first It was a just a random car driving by but within half an hour the streets were filled with cars driving round and round the block, drivers tooting their horns and passengers screaming out of the windows. It went on until some time after 1 am. I went to sleep sometime after 2am.

15 Radiotherapy: The Second Half

The Big Scary Machine isn't scary any more, becoming Billy No Mates getting lucky with the super-hot titty syndrome, saint to sinner in less than 12 hours, evidence of people a lot worse off than me, a new barrier that isn't language and how not to break good news.

July 7ᵗʰ

Himself sent me a message reminding me I was half-way through already. This gave me cause to review where I was.

Firstly, the Big Scary Machine was, by now, not even a bit scary. It was just the machine. All lower case. If anything, I was feeling quite affectionate towards it. Every time a new bit hove into view I got quite excited.

Secondly, everybody I knew who had had radiotherapy for breast cancer had told me how important the cream was. I thought they must be right because I was applying it morning and evening and had had no ill effects. My difference was that I never once felt like I needed to put it on; I just did. By now my right breast definitely appeared to be pinker than the other. It looked like a slight case of sunburn but no worse than that. It was warm to the touch but never hot like it had been after the test session. It looked like I was completely escaping the super-hot titty syndrome.

The third thing people had told me[21] was that I would be waiting around a lot. That simply didn't happen. Every appointment I had had was either exactly on time or early, until, strangely enough, this day. On this day I had arrived on time and the woman ahead of me (the tall beautiful one) hadn't yet gone in. We were 15 minutes late. I could live with that.

The fourth and final thing was that the radiotherapy machine didn't always follow the same pattern. Occasionally It would take slightly longer and this day – the first day of the latter part of my treatment - a bit of it'd never seen before suddenly swang into view. It was like a mechanical octopus. I gave it Ottavius as a pet name; Otty for short.

-0-

There was a massive supermarket opposite Leo's flat

---

[21] This is people in the UK, not in Italy. The punctuality in Italy might have been a consequence of Covid and the need to keep people separated. Certainly. the notice I had read earlier implied that punctuality wasn't necessarily the norm.

and I went in there every day to buy fresh food. One evening, waiting in the queue staring into space and not paying attention, I became slowly aware that it was taking a long time. I realised, belatedly, that the woman in front of me was putting items back because she didn't have enough money. When she put the third or fourth thing back I asked the cashier how much she still needed. It was only about 5 Euros so I gave the money to the cashier – as would anyone in that situation. The woman thanked me fulsomely and when I came out of the supermarket she was waiting there to thank me again. I said "You don't have to thank me. It's only 5 euros. Really, it's nothing". Then she started crying. I don't mean a few tears. I mean really crying.

This was awful. I couldn't hug her (Covid) so I handed her a tissue and suggested we go for a coffee. Almost immediately I realised that was a stupid thing to say as she had no money. I rephrased it to let me give you a coffee.

In the bar not 50 metres away, she told me her story. Born in Poland she had come to Italy about 20 years ago, married and settled. Since her marriage broke down some years ago it has been just her and her teenage daughter, so she started cleaning work to pay the bills. She told me she worked 'all the time' but sometimes, 'like today', she did not have enough money to buy what they needed. Listening to her made me realise just how lucky I was. I mean, I knew anyway, but it doesn't hurt to be reminded now and then.

-0-

The next day my halo didn't so much slip as crash to the floor and shatter. I have a bad habit of being lost in my own word and oblivious to my surroundings. If I tell you that I was

184

once in a gym, on a machine next to the machine my husband was on, and I never even noticed him there, you'll get an idea of how dozy I can be.

This time I was leaving the apartment building just as a man was coming in. He said Buon Giorno to me and I ignored him. That's right. I ignored him. In Italy (or certainly in Abruzzo) that's a cardinal sin. Everybody says Buon Giono and you said Buon Giorno back. That's the unwritten, inviolate rule. He was outraged.

"Signora" he shouted at me. I don't exaggerate - he really did shout.

I woke up and looked at him. "Scusa?" I asked.

"You were very rude to me. I said Buon Giorno to you".

I was mortified. "I'm sorry" I stammered out, "Buon Giorno" but it was too late, he had me labelled as rude and ignorant and hissed 'maleducato' at me as he pushed through the door[22]. It shouldn't have mattered but it was on my mind as I walked to the hospital. That day I made an extra effort to said hello to everyone as I arrived and thank you as I left. Even to the receptionists safely behind their glass.

-0-

I tried walking along the beach. It was cooler, but not much. It was very crowded even at 6pm, and it's a torture being on a beach and not being allowed to sunbathe. The river

---

[22] It could have been worse. He could have said 'stronza'. Then I would have been mortified for days.

was better and more interesting.

-0-

On Thursday I was outside the changing cubicle, changed into my gown waiting to be called through, when I noticed that the storage room next door had changed. It had used to be full of files and general office detritus but now it had shelves on every wall containing what looked like bits of tailor dummies. Nobody was looking so I went in to investigate.

Every shelf carried a row of face/head masks in mesh. Some were clearly constructed to cover the torso and head, others just the neck and head. They were all labelled with a name and a date and had marks which indicated where the radiotherapy beam would be directed. There were screw holes where the masks were bolted to the table to make sure the patient stayed absolutely still[23]. I couldn't think of anything more claustrophobic and terrifying. I still can't.

-0-

When it got to Friday I was up early. Being right in the centre of Pescara had encouraged me to do quite a bit of unnecessary shopping so I had a lot more to pack than I came with.

I cleaned the apartment (including the whiteboard which I had covered with notes) and put all my bags in the hallway ready to leave, before going out and buying a gift bag for the three bottles of one (red, rosé and white, I didn't know which

---

[23] These were my assumptions about the purpose of the screw holes and bits of tape. I think I was right though.

he preferred) I'd bought as a thank you for Leo. I placed the bag in the centre of the table. It was time to go to the hospital for the last session of the week.

When I came out of the hospital Himself was there waiting for me. We found a bar for lunch then went back to Leo's place to pick up my stuff. We parked the car in the private barriered car park, as close to his apartment block as possible then carried all my stuff down in shifts. When it was all finally stowed in the car, I went back up the two flights of stairs to give the apartment one last check over. Everything was exactly as it should be, so I put the keys onto the table, next to my thank you note and left, and closing the door behind me. I gave it a push to double check that it had locked properly behind me and went back down to the car.

Himself had already moved out from the parking space so I got into the car, and we drove towards the exit. Only then did either of us remember the automatic metal barrier that controlled the entrance/exit. More specifically, we remembered that the remote control that operated the barrier was on the bunch of keys that I'd just locked in the apartment.

Bummer.

The only thing I could think of was asking the people in the apartment next door ... except we weren't sure if they were even in, plus we couldn't get back onto the building. Leo wasn't due back in Pescara at least 3 hours and I really, really wanted to go home. After a while we decided the best solution would be to ring doorbells and hope someone might buzz us into the main entrance. Yes, it was a long shot, but at least then we could try the people who may or may not be in Leo's other apartment. The front entrance was out of the car park and a 2-

or 3-minute walk around the block so Himself left me with the car and set off alone.

Himself had been gone about 5 minutes when the barrier rose, and a man drove in. Before he could get out of his car I was there, tapping on his window. Accosting strangers used to be a real hurdle for me but being lost in hospital mazes about to be late for crucial appointments had hardened me up no end.

Trying to convince him of our credentials (I'm not a burglar, honest) I made the mistake of over explaining, which confused him. He thought I want to use his keys to get back into the apartment block and, as he said, he lived in the block opposite. When I clarified that it was just the barrier I needed lifting he was more than happy to help, but not before extracting a conversation as payment. 'What was I doing in Pescara? he asked. 'How long had I lived in Italy? Did I know London? How about Dublin? Did I know Dublin?' That was a bit left field but I said yes I did at which point he switched to English.

"I worked in Dublin for three years" he told me. 'At the University. Do you know it?"

Just then Himself came back and he too joined the conversation. It was another twenty minutes before we actually got to opening the barrier and leaving.

-0-

At home I received a massive bunch of flowers from my brother-in-law and his wife back in the U.K. They were beautiful and I was annoyed that I had to leave them there when I went back to Pescara.

July 12ᵗʰ – July 16ᵗʰ (therapy days 13 – 17)

Every Airbnb in Pescara was booked up, so I was forced into a hotel for my final week and a half. That was the disadvantage of a popular seaside town in high summer.

The upside of the hotel was air conditioning and reliable internet (useful for my Microsoft Team meetings). The downside was the lack of a restaurant. I'd have to eat out every night looking like Billy No mates, and the nights would be very long.

-0-

Back at the hospital they had changed the route to the treatment room. Which would have been fine except that nobody forewarned me. When my number came up on the screen and I was met with a closed door and a sign saying Strictly No Admittance I panicked a bit. Quite a lot really. As ever there was no one around to ask and I faffed about for ages debating whether I should go back through to reception and ask them (would I get back in?). I was just about to risk it when I heard a voice with more than a hint of impatience in it calling my name. A nurse stood the far end of the corridor waving at me. Belatedly, I noticed the new sign saying changing room in very big letters with a massive arrow pointing the way.

The new route took me through the horror mask room and I confess that I took a sneak peek every time I went through, trembling for the poor sods who had to go through that treatment.

CANCER WITHOUT SUBTITLES

-0-

This week, more than halfway through my treatment, was when I belatedly realised that the numbered tickets had additional information on them, like how many people were ahead of you in the queue. When I checked back on my old tickets (yes I am that sad, I had kept them) I realised that they also said things like your appointment is not for 30 minutes, please wait in the corridor. I knew exactly which date that related to. No wonder he'd looked at me like I was an idiot.

-0-

I had pretty much cleared Pescara out for shopping so I was just wandering the streets now. There was an art exhibition 'Trash People' in the main square which I visited several times. I also became a lunch regular at the bar around the corner from the hotel, although I still didn't want to eat alone at night. Fortunately I discovered a supermarket en-route from the hospital that that sold restaurant grade salmon and tuna for sushi. Once I knew that I stocked up on soy sauce and Japanese mustard and most nights found me in my room eating sashimi. Luckily I love sashimi.

-0-

Everything got better on the Tuesday. It being himself's birthday he came to stay overnight.

I had company! Billy had mates! It was brilliant!

He wanted to eat zabaglione so we crossed the river to go to a bar he particularly likes and then to his favourite restaurant – where he decided he didn't want zabaglione after all. To be fair, by the time we'd ploughed our way through the main meal, neither did I. We still struggle with the quantity of restaurant food served in Italy[24] and this food was rich too.

It was such a fabulous evening I didn't want it to end. We were still wandering the warm streets at midnight and could almost imagine we were on holiday. Which was a much better feeling than being there for cancer treatment.

-0-

The next day at the hospital was my first ever with any serious delay. When I arrived, my ticket and the electronic screen told me there were 6 people waiting in the queue ahead of me and my heart sank. The waiting room was as empty as ever but I could spot a few people on stretchers in the corridor so I resigned myself to waiting hours. Slightly more than 30 minutes later someone came to collect me. It transpired that the screen was malfunctioning; checking people in but not advancing the numbers when people left. It didn't explain the people on stretchers though.

-0-

The day after was a real whizzbanger of a radiotherapy session. It was far longer than usual and instead of just the overhead section, I met all the other parts of the machine. I wondered if this stepping up to a final boost where they would fry my titty completely. If I'd had the language skills I would have asked.

July 19th – 23rd (therapy days 18 & 19)

---

[24] It's not just restaurant food. Every trip to a person's house involves food too. It's no wonder I'd put weight on.

Going back to the hotel for the final three days felt like a real hardship. Himself had promised to come and stay overnight on Tuesday so that we could go to the final appointment together, and then straight home. I couldn't wait for Wednesday to come.

-0-

Monday was a high day for the hospital staff. Italy had just won the world cup, beating England on penalties.

"Was I very sad that England had been beaten?" they asked me as they were positioning me on the table.

"No" I replied. "I thought the better team won". Given that they were operating the death ray machine I thought being gracious in defeat was the wisest option.

-0-

That night I began to worry that maybe I'd misunderstood and the treatment wasn't 20 days. I was thinking that maybe it would go on longer and it was really bugging me. On the Tuesday morning I woke up determined to ask the technician. If Wednesday wasn't my last day I wanted to know beforehand so I could be prepared.

I didn't get the chance. As the nurse was lowering my bed post-treatment she told me the doctor wanted to speak to me. I was to go to the waiting room after I had dressed and she'd collect me. I did, and after waiting there about 10 minutes she arrived and took me to the small office opposite. Here, a doctor I hadn't seen before was entering data into a computer. I squinted at the file and saw my name on it.

I sat in silence for roughly fifteen minutes while he wrote and then rewrote something. At one point he turned and asked me a question. I scrambled to decipher what he had said and isolated the words 'painful' and 'side effects'.

"No" I said "There wasn't any. No pain, Well, only the tiniest bit, so not really pain at all. Il dolore era piccolissimo".

He looked at me more closely. "Ah yes" he said "You're the inglese".

"Yes I am". I said in Italian in my well-practised way. "But don't worry, if you speak to me slowly I understand".

He smiled and nodded but I noticed he didn't ask me any more direct questions.

Finally he finished what he was doing and printed something off. He read it, signed it and passed it to me. It was the summary of my treatment.

I looked at it, confused. "Am I finished?" I asked.

"Yes" he said.

"What? My treatment is finished? All finished? Everything?"

" Yes" he affirmed again.

"So I don't have to come here tomorrow?" (I know I was sounding like an idiot now, but I had to be sure).[25]

---

[25] When I got home I realised I still had the hospital gown that was 'mine for the duration'. I think I'll post it back anonymously.

193

"Yes" he said with the subtlest of sighs. "The therapy is finished. This is your report. Would you like another copy for your doctor?"

"Yes please" I said, and he printed and signed another copy.

"Thank you" I said. "Thank you so much for everything". "It was our pleasure" he replied, and he actually meant it.

Walking out I was almost through the door of Radiotherapy for the last time when I let it swing shut and went back to the reception desk. "Thank you" I said. "Thank you so much for everything". "It was our pleasure" they said, and they meant it.

Outside in the corridor there was a woman, sitting alone, waiting, and looking terrified. "Don't worry" I told her. "Everyone is very kind, and the therapy is very easy". And I meant it.

-0-

I was still in the hospital grounds when I called himself. He was at home.

"I've got good news and bad news" I said blithely, not for one second thinking about how those words might sound to him.

"The bad news is I've already booked the hotel room. The good news is the treatment finished today".

He was torn between shouting at me for scaring him

194

half to death and being happy that it was over. He chose happy.

16 POST RADIOTHERAPY

Roses, a surprise party, more treatments, the mysterious shrinking titty, another new friend, failing at yoga, more stuff I didn't know, bolshy blood-takers, a personal diet and exercise plan, and yet another ultrasound in yet another hospital.

June 24th

When we got home there was a rose bush on the doorstep to say congratulations. It was from two of our friends. The next day there was a second rose bush, from two other friends. I hadn't really thought of the radiotherapy as being a big deal, so I was really touched to be given gifts. I felt like a fraud.

June 27th

A few days later I felt like even more of a fraud when I walked into a surprise 'congratulations it's all over' party. I'd never had a surprise party before. I'd like to think I took it in my stride, looking dead cool and sophisticated. The reality is I started to cry as soon as I spotted all the balloons and people and realised what was going on.

July 31st - August 4th

More surprises. A birthday trip to Rome.

August 6th

I contacted the integrated medicine team to reschedule my appointments. We agreed on dates in October as I hoped to go back to the UK in September. (In the event, thanks to the UK's Covid resurgence I didn't, but I left the appointments where they were).

On the advice of a friend, I began taking supplements, specifically magnesium, calcium and sea buckthorn oil with Omega 7. They made a difference to the side effects of the Letrozole. I would recommend the same thing to anyone[26].

August 14th

Against my better judgement I'd become addicted to news stories about people with a serious illness. I think it was a 'there but for the grace of God' type thing. This day I read a story in the news about a woman in the UK whose husband died because of untreated gall stones. It was awful. A genuine tragedy. He had tried to see his GP but been refused a face to face appointment and was only taken to hospital after he collapsed with pain. He died before an operation could be scheduled because, according to his wife, the hospitals were overloaded with Covid. She said he was just as much a victim of the Covid pandemic as people who died from Covid and that - these were her exact words - "He was my beloved

---

[26] Seabuckthorm Oil /Omega 7 is impossible to source in Italy. I order it online from Holland & Barret in Ireland, thus avoiding customs charges.

husband and a precious father. He wasn't just a statistic".

I thought, not for the first time, how lucky I was to be here in Italy when I was diagnosed. Never once had I felt like 'just a statistic'. To be fair, I don't think cancer patients in the UK feel like statistics either – I've never heard anyone complain about a lack of compassion in their care. No, I was talking about what happens at the primary care level.

An example: A few months after my operation I went to get my prescription renewed. I went to the surgery without an appointment because that's what you do in my little commune. While I was waiting in the ante-room the doctor came out (to take some air) and we had a conversation. It was nothing specific, just general and friendly ('Hi, how's it going? are you having any problems? isn't it hot today? did you want to see me?' etc), but it made me remember my doctor back in Sevenoaks who needed my notes in front of her to even know who I was. That's not a criticism of my doctor in Sevenoaks – I was rarely ill and would always agree to see any doctor in the practise for expediency, so I doubt I met her more than 5 times in 15 years. My next experience of primary care was in Margate and that was something else. There, the doctors were disinterested and dismissive to the point of rudeness. It was also so hard to get an appointment with one of them that, more often than not, you gave up before being seen.

Anyway, I've digressed. Back to my example.

When it was my turn for the dispensary I went in and had a similar but longer conversation with the woman dispensing the prescriptions, who also happens to be the doctor's wife. Sometimes its Cara doing it, other times it's her mother Serena. At that time I had only ever met Serena twice, and apprehension about the language barrier had stilted our conversations. This time, it was different. After apologising for not being her (English speaking) daughter aka my saviour Cara, Serena told me how much Cara had worried about me and how often she talked about me. When I eventually left, prescriptions in hand, she even blew me kisses through her mask in lieu of cheek kissing. I realised then that the formal barriers of language and medic/patient had both fallen while I wasn't even there, kicked over by Cara. I was still a patient, but now I was a real person too.

August 16th

It was a determined sort of day. 6 months since I last did any yoga and over 2 months since I announced I was going to resume (ha!). I got my yoga mat out. Sick of tired of feeling stiff and achy all the time, I was fired up to do something about it. I especially wanted to get rid of the horrible stiff ankles and feet I now habitually woke up with. I didn't know if this was connected to the medication, but never having had it before, I assumed it was. I put it on my list of things to ask when I got to my Medicine Integrata consultation.

I'd identified the course of 30 daily yoga lesson I was going to follow. I'd done the course once before so I knew it would be perfect. The first lessons were really easy, very basic yoga, only gradually building to something more challenging.

Two minutes in, sitting upright and breathing, I was congratulating myself on a good decision.

10 minutes in, sweating so hard that my hands were slipping off the mat I was questioning my judgement.

15 minutes in, a simple arm lift combined with an easy side-lean made muscles I didn't know I had scream in protest. I was beginning to realise just how weak and feeble I'd become.

20 minutes in, struggling through a side lunge movement, I was distracted by the flab on my thigh. Where the hell had that come from?

I got through to the end and every part of me knew I'd been exercising. I was worried. Day one of the programme, which I used to dismiss as the 'waste of time because pretty much all you do is breathe' session, had half killed me.

August 20th

I switched to an easier yoga lesson. Shorter and with fewer exercises that required arm strength.

August 23rd

I downgraded the yoga again.

August 25th

And again.

August 26th

And again. This was the final downgrade. I decided on just 10 minutes of very easy stretching yoga and only every other day. It wasn't just me being lazy – it was making my arms and shoulder hurt too much.

I was also going on a better eating regime for the flab.

August 27th

Doing my regular 'how's my scar coming along' check in the mirror I noticed that my right breast was now definitely smaller than my left breast. It was one of the things I was told might happen with radiotherapy but of course I didn't think it would happen to me. It's not a common side effect. Maybe it was to balance out me not suffering titty burn. Cancer karma.

When I say smaller, it wasn't a massive difference, but it was noticeable. At least it was to me. And still is. I decided to leave it for a while, but I was already thinking of strategies to disguise it. My initial thought was to revert to my 13 years-old self and stuff cotton wool inside my bra. Then I thought I might buy padded bras and just take the padding out on one side[27].

September

A hedonistic month with short trips to Termoli and Florence. Given that the beach had been forbidden all summer (radiotherapy and sun exposure don't mix for a year after treatment) it was indescribably good to have a spot of self-indulgence. Unfortunately, after just a week in Florence my ear was out of tune with the Abruzzo accent. I was finding it hard to decipher what people were saying to me. Again.

October 4th

I called Cara. With my integrated medicine appointment just a week away I needed to book a blood test. Given that my 6-

---

[27] In the end I did neither. It really isn't that big a deal and I doubt anyone other than me (and maybe himself if he's paying attention) has even noticed.

month check was due not long after, it made sense to book all my pre-check tests at the same time.

Cara said not to worry about coming to the surgery — she would come to me. Which she did and which was when I discovered that I still hadn't cracked this whole hospital thing at all.

Prescriptions apparently last a month. As a consequence, all the prescriptions for the pre-check-up scans, given to me back in April, were now out of date. I should have forward booked the tests immediately, not filed them away to do later. Now Cara would have to reissue them.

You know that really small feeling you get when you've done something obviously stupid? That's the feeling I had, and it had an alarming effect on my confidence. In seconds, it had crashed back to rock-bottom. I had thought I was over the pre appointments anxiety but it was back again, in spades

October 6th

Medicine Integrata emailed me to move the time of my appointment. I didn't mind. If they had moved the date I would have. I knew this part of the treatment was optional but to me it was important. I think it being optional made it feel like it was me doing something positive for myself, rather than other people fixing things for me.

October 8th

I got to the clinic for my blood tests and my name wasn't on the list. It didn't really matter but it was clearly a source of irritation and the nurse who took my blood was consequently brusque. She handed me a piece of paper which said I could get the results the following Wednesday

I asked if I could get them online, but no "we don't do that here" she said. I explained that it was a problem for me because I needed the results for the Tuesday,

"Could I phone earlier?" I asked.

"No" she said impatiently, "in fact they might not be ready on Wednesday. It's just an approximate date".

"But I need them for Tuesday"

She mumbled something about talking to my doctor. She then told her colleagues (in Italian) that I didn't understand what she saying because I was English, implying that I was being a right pain in the butt – which I probably was. To me she started to enunciate very clearly with exaggerated gestures, telling me to hold the cotton pad in place and wait 5 minutes in the dressing room before leaving.

I didn't interrupt or tell her that I had understood everything she said perfectly because what was the point? She was only the second "brusque" person I'd met on this journey and I hoped that she would be the last, but it showed that every health system has one thing in common. People. And people are not always who you would like them to be.

October 12th

It was time for my appointment with Medicine Integrata. My doctor had phoned for my blood test results but got the same blank wall I had crashed into, so I would just have to apologise and promise to email them later. I also had a cold but I didn't want to postpone the appointment so I loaded myself up with cold cures and went anyway. As instructed, I was bathed, free of any body lotions, not wearing tights and fasting. I couldn't eat or drink anything within two hours of the appointment. I was ready.

We got to Ortona hospital well ahead of my appointment time because I needed to go to the CUP and change my ricetta for an authorisation. As I knew, the CUP could take as little as 5 minutes or as much as an hour and I didn't want to be late. Add to that a dose of translation paranoia and a husband who is positively anal about being punctual and you'll have an idea of how early we were.

The CUP was closed. It closed at 5pm and it was now 5.15pm. My appointment was at 6. Damn. I was stuffed. I decided to go upstairs and find the waiting room anyway. I'd driven an hour to get there (or at least Himself had) so I had to at least try. At this point I should say that I was happy to drive there myself but Himself insisted. He said he'd been with me every step so far and wanted to carry on being with me.

There were several couples in the waiting room. Once again, I was the only one still observing the no partners rule. They left one by one (two by two) and I read the posters on the wall for something to do. I'd just zapped a bar code on a poster for more information on acupuncture (which I really wanted to know about) when a doctor arrived and asked my name. It seemed the person ahead of me hadn't arrived so he took me in early instead.

The first thing he said sounded something like I had to do something or did I have something? What? The word I hadn't grabbed sounded something like impegnativo which in turn sounded like something to do with working.

I made a wild stab and guessed he was asking for the work authorisation. "No" I said "I'm sorry but the CUP was closed. Is it a problem?" I guessed good because he said no, I could just bring it with me the next time. I was on a roll now, so I told him that I didn't have the blood results either. That also was not a problem. Today, he said, was all about establishing a baseline.

We begin filling in the habitual pile of forms and I handed him my post-surgery notes authorizing my treatment. He transferred bits of information, but I had no idea what they were, and asked some supplementary questions. We soon segued into the fact that I was English.

"Had you ever lived in London?" he asked.

"Yes, for ten years".

"Where?"

"Blackheath". He didn't know Blackheath.

"It's near Greenwich" I told him. He still didn't know it. He then told me that he had lived in Regents Park for 2 years and that explained everything.

"That's why you don't know Greenwich and Blackheath" I told him. "You were over in the posh bit".

Posh took a bit of translating.

-0-

We stopped just before the signatures so that could tell

me what Medicine Integrata was about. He was at pains to stress that it was not in any way a replacement for the medicines I was taking or any traditional cancer treatment. It was about dealing with the stress that cancer can cause and the mental and physical problems that can arise from that. He talked about positive and negative stress and cortisone levels which I could follow, but mainly because I already knew something about the subject. If I didn't, I think I would have been lost because the more enthusiastic he got (and he was very enthusiastic) about his subject, the faster he talked. His hands were a blur by the end.

Today, I was told, they would do measurement and analysis and then I had things to do and then some more tests and then after that I would be given advice on lifestyle and diet. Did I understand? Yes. Was I happy? Yes. Did I consent to the treatment? Yes. Did I consent to my data being used for research? Yes. In that case I should sign here and here.

I signed.

He left the room briefly, came back and invited me into a second room. Here, there was a young, slim, rather beautiful girl, all dressed in black who I assumed to be the nutritionist. (I later found out I was wrong – she was just there to do some tests). There were more forms to complete, but this time it was minimal. I took my boots and socks off [28] so she could weigh me. She measured my height and noted that down too. Next, I lay on the examination couch while she attached electrodes to my hands and feet. She told me this was to measure my body composition.

---

[28] It had turned from summer into winter in just one week and I was feeling the cold.

After the electrodes, she measured me every which way. I made a point of not looking at what she was writing because I really didn't want to know. Since having cancer I'd taken minimal exercise and the weight had accumulated. I know this because the jeans I was wearing were tight and I had a belly bulge over the top. I'm not saying I was slim before. Pre cancer I definitely had a muffin top but now I had a whole bakery store. It was gross and it had to go.

Socks and shoes back on she told me what would happen. First, I had a thing that looked like a watch to wear, for tracking my activity, sleep etc. it was actually like a really chunky Fitbit except it was completely blank and had no buttons I could push to see how I was getting on. I had to wear this continually except for when I showered.

Secondly, I had to keep a food diary listing everything I ate and drank each day, along with the time of consumption, quantities, where I was consuming it and any other relevant information (like boredom eating etc). Rather than have all the faff of weighing the foods she gave me a food chart which showed different size food servings on plates with an indication of how many grammes they were. It was a very Italian food chart: nothing on there even vaguely resembled processed food. Every portion was either plain meat, pasta or vegetables.

I also had to keep a diary of any exercise I took and make a note of when I took the bracelet on and off. That was it. They would see me again in 9 days.

October 21st

The 2nd time I went to Medicine Integrata, the CUP was open. From the authorisation they gave me I saw that the cost of my appointments was slightly less than fifty euros. That's under Italy's subsidised health system. I thought that was a real bargain. Of course, I was paying nothing at all, which was even more of a bargain.

-0-

I'd only been in the waiting room a few minutes when a very tall man came in and asked for my bracelet and sleep diary. He took them away and I was left alone. At first, I whiled the time away by running the information posters through google translate and saving them as notes on my phone. I thought they might be useful, but I've never looked at them since, partly because the next 90 minutes pre-empted everything they had to say.

Then a woman – another patient - came in and began to talk to me. It was at machine gun pace so I asked her to slow down and, miracle of miracles she did. At last, a conversation with a stranger that I could understand. As a consequence, when the doctor (female, blonde enviably slim) arrived to fetch me I was unfazed by her lack of English. I could do this I told myself. Nonetheless I pulled my phone out of my pocket. A little bit of Google backup never hurts.

-0-

I sat opposite the nutritionist as she read my food diary. She flicked back and forth through it and queried one or two items, mainly because of my handwriting and scribbled out bits (a few times I forgot it was all supposed to be in Italian so had to cross things out and rewrite them).

"What on earth" she wanted to know, "does this say? It seems to say tea with milk".

I explained about the English stye of tea and she looked a bit sick. We discussed my (apparently strange) aversion to eating breakfast and the lack of fruit in my diet. I thought this latter was a bit unfair because if we had done the same exercise just a month before, my diary would had have been packed with fruit. Now that autumn had arrived the fruits I love eating were no longer in season and it Italy, out of season food means not available to eat food.

Then she commented on my 'sweet tooth'. I thought that was even more unfair. I told her indignantly that I don't have a sweet tooth. She raised her eyebrows and looked over her glasses at me. "Tuesday", she read from my notes "snickers bar. Wednesday, 2 Mon Cheri chocolatini), Thursday, cream filled biscotti, Sunday[29], semi freddo..."

Oh well, if she was going to use evidence! I protested that these were an exception, not my norm but she clearly wasn't convinced.

Perhaps making a causal link, she moved onto my weight. Had I put weight on? I knew I was heavier than I had been, but I couldn't tell her by how much because I've never really weighed myself. In that case, how long had I been putting weight on? That I did know. Post-menopause certainly and more so post-operation. We both agreed that I was heavier than I should be. AKA too fat.

We talked about the foods I liked, didn't like and

---

[29] Obviously, she said all this in Italian, but it was the way she said it.

couldn't eat[30]. We talked about breakfast and what I might be persuaded to eat. She proposed rusks and I countered with toast. I proposed boiled eggs and she countered with scrambled. She joked that I couldn't have bacon and eggs. I feigned insult and replied that I wasn't American. With a slight shudder she conceded to allowing English tea at breakfast. We were both struggling for a third option when I remembered I like porridge. She agreed porridge was good and added it to the list.

Before very long we had finished. She was going to prepare and email me a diet to follow 'which I must follow exactly ' and then I would have a follow up review in a months' time. Now I had to go back to the waiting room before part two on exercise and sleep. I assumed this would be with the tall man who had taken my watch.

-0-

Alone in the waiting room again a man arrived and asked me something. I didn't catch it but I was full of confidence now, so I just asked him to repeat it. After he'd repeated it three times (the third time removing his mask in an effort to be understood) I gave up and told him I couldn't help. I still haven't got the faintest clue what he was saying.

-0-

I was right. It was the tall man who did exercise and sleep. After a shaky start where I failed on every third sentence

---

[30] Allergies not fussiness.

he asked if he could take his mask off to make communication easier. I readily agreed and we were fine after that. Not because I was any better at understanding but because he turned out to have a decent level of English.

My results were fascinating. My sleep was even worse than I knew it to be. I had thought that I was hitting deep sleep at some points but according to my monitor I hardly ever got to the deep sleep stage. That meant my cortisone levels weren't ever decreasing, which meant bits of me weren't repairing properly. He said it was probably why I got up in a bad mood most mornings (cheek, but he was right).

I also had a high level of anxiety. It was not quite high enough for an automatic referral, but he offered psychological support if I wanted it. I said no, because the thought of tackling a counselling session in Italian was enough to make my anxiety go through the roof. Besides, I didn't feel anxious even if my body was saying I was. Although by then of course, I was feeling anxious about the fact that I was apparently feeling anxious without knowing that I was feeling anxious.

Finally, he told me that I was too sedentary and the fat distribution on my body, being all round my stomach, was skewed. The rest of me seemed in pretty good nick though, and my muscle tone got a special mention. Small cheer for me.

I got points for doing yoga every day (now up to a whole 15 minutes) but he wanted me to do 10 minutes of relaxing yoga at night too, in the hour before I went to bed. That would help me sleep. The diet I was being given would also help, but it was important I kept to it and didn't start swapping lunches and dinners around. In addition, I needed to do some proper exercise at least 4 times a week.

When I blanched at the thought, he said that going for a long walk would do, especially as I lived in the countryside. Did I know that blues and greens were good colours for helping with anxiety? Well, they are, and being able to walk in the countryside easily meant I had no excuse not to. Finally. I had to get up and move around for ten minutes in every sixty by which he means proper moving "just doing housework isn't enough". I hadn't the heart to tell him that I was far too lazy to do regular housework.

To my utter delight he asked if I might be interested in acupuncture. I tried to be cool but I think my shrill "Siii, Grazie!!" in response might have blown that idea. He offered to book me in. It would be a session every two weeks and four sessions in total. It looked like it would not be until January but if he could get me in earlier he would. I was thrilled.

Collectively everything was designed to stop the hot flashes I was getting, ease the joint pain (I hadn't mentioned this, but he seemed to know about it anyway[31]), improve my shitty sleep and get rid of my flabby middle. I am, of course, paraphrasing. He was much more polite than that.

-0-

In the evening my piano nutrizionale (aka eating plan) arrived from the nutritionist. it was strange because it looked both impossibly strict and actually quite appealing at the same time. It also assumed a ready access to fresh ingredients and the intention to prepare and cook food yourself, twice a day. I was not sure it would work in England. Anyway, the proof would be in the eating as they say.

---

[31] As it's a common side effect of Letrozolo that makes sense to me

October 24th

Medicine Integrata invited me to a zoom meeting. So far as I understood, it was a support group where we all discussed issues and shared experiences. I tried but after 40 minutes of sharing (listening) I'd had enough. Zoom and the Italian race are not a match made in heaven because Italians really like to talk, and preferably all at the same time. These women particularly liked to talk. When they started comparing childhood diets in Puglia and Emilia Romagna, I decided enough was enough. My ears hurt from the volume and my brain hurt from trying and failing to keep up.

Me and Himself we went out for an over-boozy night out with friends instead. It was my last indulgence before I embraced my new healthy lifestyle.

October 26th

I made a list of all the diet ingredients and went shopping. So far so good. 2 days in, apart from having to eat breakfast which felt alien to me, the meals I was preparing were actually really good. So good that Himself abandoned his own lunch plans to eat the same thing.

October 27th

My first official check-up was looming, so I was having another upper body ultrasound. This hospital (number 5) is a private one, just outside Chieti. Google Maps told us the journey would take 65 minutes so Himself had allowed 100. Didn't want to be late.

Minutes before we were due to leave a man phoned us

to say that he was arriving with 144 sacks of wood pellets.

"When?" we asked.

"Now" he said.

He was parked outside our house.

-0-

By the time we were on the road Himself was a bit edgy. Throughout the whole journey we were worrying about being late and only really relaxed when we arrived in the car park. Half an hour early.

Being Covid careful, we waited in the car for 15 minutes. It was a nice car park. I think I could have guessed this was a private hospital because it had actual spaces, by which I mean parking spaces marked out as well as empty spaces. It was the first hospital car park I'd been in that didn't require you to breathe in as you drove between the double-parked cars.

With fifteen minutes left, we both went to the front door. Me for my appointment and him because he thought he'd go inside to get a coffee. By now I was well accustomed to the temperature monitoring machines at every entrance but this one was manned by two nurses, monitoring the monitoring machine. We were about the 4th in the queue to go in. When it was my turn, the machine wouldn't read my temperature.

"Step forward" the nurses told me.

"No step back".

"No forward".

"A bit more back".

"Crouch down, your head needs to be inside the outline".

I did all of those (more than once) with no joy. Eventually they measured my temperature with a hand-held device.

At least I got inside. Himself, not being a patient, wasn't allowed to put a foot inside the door.

-0-

If I thought the car park was flash the reception was something else. Deep chesterfield sofas in brown leather lined the walls and the CUP, clad in oak, was like the reception of a five-star hotel. It was a far cry from the system at Chieti which reminded me of a city centre jobcentre.

That's where the differences ended. The waiting to register was exactly the same.

I took a ticket from the machine (hopefully from the right category) and checked it. It said I was C83 and 6th in the queue. That's not so bad I thought. Except there was also an H queue, an A queue and a P queue. H seems to be the most popular number to be called and C the least popular. At about 15 seconds before my appointment time I went back to the nurse/sentry at the door and asked if I needed to wait for the CUP as I already had a confirmed appointment. Apparently I did as otherwise I wouldn't be checked in.

I was desperate for the toilet now too, but I daren't leave in case my number was called. If I missed it I'd have to take another ticket and start again.

Finally, 10 minutes after my scheduled appointment time and 25 minutes after I walked through door it was my turn. Now I discovered why it had been taking so long. I had to complete yet another registration form (name, age place of birth, date of birth current address, codice fiscale etc) and sign various bits of paper, all of which had to be photocopied. Given a pen I could easily had completed this form while I was waiting but I guess that would have been far too easy

I was directed to the radiotherapy area (follow the yellow lines on the floor) and when I got there a doctor was hovering, waiting for me He didn't look best pleased with me if I'm honest. We went into an individual consulting room and he asked for my last test results. I knew the score by now and had everything with me. He was an older doctor than I was used to seeing and it suddenly struck me how relatively young all my carers had been. I don't think any of them had seen the back of their 40s. It's a big job and must take an enormous toll on them. This was clearly a gentler pace of work and I guessed it was a type of semi-retirement for him.

He was very thorough. I took my top off and lay on the gurney to be splodged with cold goo. From then on he said nothing more than breathe in, hold and relax as he moved me into different positions and slid the scanning apparatus over me, pressing down in some places, just as the last doctor had. The pressing down bit always coincides with the take a deep breath and hold it instruction, which makes holding your breath for so long even harder than it would normally be. I know I've already mentioned that, but they seemed to be completely unaware that I was about to burst each time.

It was soon over and very much quicker than the last one. I realised that was because I'd read the instructions not to eat or drink anything for 12 hours beforehand. I must have sent that last machine really haywire.

After I dressed I waited outside and in less than 5 minutes I had my test results. He told me that everything was clear. I was less time with the doctor than I was in the waiting room.

October 28th

The results of my movement and sleep monitoring came through from medicine integrata. There were 26 pages of it which tied my evening up nicely in translation. I needn't really have bothered because it was everything he had already told me: my sleep was appalling; I was so physically inactive I made a sloth look like Mo Farah and I need to do something about it now. Like, right now. Fortunately, what to do about it was also included, plus directions to a relaxation app I should download and use.

17 THE 6 MONTH CHECK

Computer-sitting, a long wait, conversations with strangers, Senior & Junior make a re-appearance and ten minutes to happiness.

November 10ᵗʰ

This was the day I'd been waiting for. For some reason the 6-month check was really important. It felt like confirmation (hopefully) that they hadn't made some dreadful mistake and the cancer had really gone. Yes, I know that doesn't mean it can't come back again, or that I won't get cancer somewhere else in my body, but, as politicians like to say, it drew a line under it.

When I had had the first follow up appointment in Chieti (keep up - that was the one with Senior and Junior) they had said I might not have to be there in person, and I should check beforehand. That was because of Covid, but the situation had eased a lot since then and, despite any inconvenience, I really wanted to be told everything was okay in person. Note I was assuming that everything would be okay. There was a teeny tiny part of my brain saying 'what if it isn't' but I wasn't listening to that.

The phone call was made, and it was confirmed that I should go in person. Yay!

-0-

One slight problem. I had a new computer scheduled to arrive on the 11th, and, in the afternoon of the 9th I got an email saying it would be arriving a day early. There was absolutely no way of getting in touch with the suppliers to say don't deliver it I won't be here. Normally I would have left a note saying to leave the delivery 'round the back' but it was peeing down with rain and predicted to carry on raining the whole of the next day. Leaving a delivery outside wasn't an option when said delivery had electronics inside it[32]. Neither was staying home to receive it.

Fortunately, just as Himself was about to reluctantly agree to stay at home, our friends Marco and Gemma offered to come over and delivery-sit until we got back. We assured them it would be a couple of hours. Maybe three. Three and a half at most.

-0-

This time when I arrived at Chieti's oncology unit the waiting room was packed. When I say packed, I mean in a socially distanced sort of way, but it was a sharp contrast to the empty room I'd been greeted with the past few times.

---

[32] I know what you're thinking but trust me, you wouldn't believe the things we've had sitting outside our house all day with no danger of them being stolen. Crates of wine, bags of pellets, electrical goods. It'll happen one day for sure ….

I reported my arrival to the receptionist who confirmed I was on the list, sat down, opened my kindle and began to wait. Yes, of course I was early. My appointment was at 1pm and it was now 12.30.

After a while I noticed that the people coming in after me were taking a ticket from one of the two machines by the reception kiosk. That worried me so I got up to look at the machines. It wasn't clear which machine you should use, or even if I needed a ticket. After all, I didn't last time, plus I had an appointment and maybe the other people didn't. I decided to ask the receptionist.

"Oh yes" she said. "You need to take a ticket", and she told me which machine to use. I was a bit peeved as at least 8 people had arrived after me and were now presumably ahead of me.

As the minutes dragged on my suspicions were confirmed. My appointment time was irrelevant. My ticket time was what mattered, and I was now almost the last person to have arrived.

I sent Himself a text to say I was waiting, and my appointment was soon.

I sent Marco and Gemma to say I was waiting. and my appointment was soon.

I read my book for a while.

I sent Himself a text telling him I'd be later than expected.

I watched tv and learned how to make French baguettes.

I sent Himself a text telling him he ought to go and get some lunch somewhere because I'd be 'a while yet'.

I called Marco and Gemma telling them to raid my fridge for food.

I put the book down and watched a tv interview with a singer who has suffered some horrible injury. I wasn't sure if it had been an accident or an illness. I think she was pretty famous, and I was supposed to already know.

I sent a Himself a text saying I was still, still waiting .

I sent Marco and Gemma a text telling them to lock up and leave if they needed to go home.

I sent someone else a text cancelling my meeting with them later that afternoon.

Every time the screen changed numbers I looked up hopefully, but the numbers shown – now all over the place – were never mine.

-0-

There was a woman sitting in the same row as me and her husband arrived to check on her. I offered to move so that he could sit with her, but he preferred to stand by the window. She took this as her cue to talk to me.

We covered a lot of ground. What was my name? What was I doing there? What operation had I had? Who did my operation? What post treatment had I had? How old was I? As a sidenote I will never get used to being asked my age by perfect strangers, but it is inevitably one of the first questions I am asked. Where did I live in England? Where did I live in Italy? What made me move to Italy? Where had I come from today? What did I do for a living? What was my ticket number? How had I travelled to the hospital? Here I somehow gave her the impression that my husband was a bus driver, and then didn't know how to correct it.

In my experience, Italians are not shy about striking up conversations with strangers, neither are they shy about eavesdropping. It's not rude, its simply being interested. If anything, it would be rude not to listen. Consequently, as I was being quizzed, I felt like we were entertaining the whole waiting room. This was confirmed after she had left, and I was once again reading my kindle. It was now 2 hours after my scheduled appointment time and I was actually reading this time, instead of looking up after every third word. I consequently missed my number finally flashing up on the screen. Seeing this the man in the row behind me, got out of his seat and came to tap me on the shoulder. "It's E83" he said, pointing at the screen. "That's your number".

-0-

I was delighted that it was the same senior doctor and junior doctor as the last time. I gave them my results, they read them, entered them into the computer, then gave me a handful of prescriptions for tests to be done before my one-year check-up. After waiting outside for 2 hours, the whole process took just 10 minutes. Everything was fine. I was fine. I could go. It really was that simple.

"Ciao" I said, "E grazie".

"Ciao" they replied. And (in English) "Happy

Christmas".

It was.

Ps. The computer arrived the next day.

18 A FINAL WORD

The six month check-up seems like a good point to end. It doesn't mean that my cancer journey is finished, and I can begin to forget about it; the medication sees to that. Every time I wake up in the night because my ankles, or my wrists or my hip is hurting I am reminded. Every time I have to move after sitting still and the bones in my feet protest, I am reminded. Every morning when I take the Letrozole tablet and a handful of herbal supplements I am reminded. Every time I put a bra on, and one cup is a tad emptier than the other I am reminded. Bizarrely the only thing that doesn't remind me daily is my scar. It is so neat and faded that I barely register it's there anymore. No, I am not finished with cancer All I hope is that it has finished with me.

MY TIMELINE

16th December
I found the lump

17th December
GP examined the lump

22nd December
Mammogram and Utrasound at Chieti Hospital

31st December
Biopsy at Chieti Hospital

12th January
Confirmed diagnosis of Breast Cancer

29th January.
First oncology consultation at Ortona Hospital (regional centre of excellence). A 2nd Ultrasound. An MRI is ordered.

2nd February
Blood tests for MRI scan

3rd February
MRI scan

13th February
Second oncology consultation at Ortona Hospital. The surgeon confirms surgery is required.

16th February
Pre-op tests at Ortona Hospital: Covid, blood, ECG, X rays.
Also consultations with the surgeons removing the lump and
the anaesthetist.

19th February
Third oncology consultation at Ortona Hospital. Measured up
by plastic surgeon for reconstructive surgery.

5th March
Covid19 test pre -operation

10th March
Operation at Ortona Hospital

12th March
Discharged from Ortona Hospital

16th March
First check up at Ortona Hospital

19th March
Second check out at Ortona Hospital

3rd April
Third check-up at Ortona Hospital. Receive recommendations
on next treatment steps.

6th April
First appointment at Oncology Clinic, Chieti Hospital. Tests
are ordered.

CANCER WITHOUT SUBTITLES

8th April
Bone Scan at Ortona Hospital

12th April
Scintigrafia Ossea at Chieti Hospital

13th April
Blood tests and ECG at Casoli Hospital

13th April
Upper body ultrasound at Chieti Hospital

14th April
Radiotherapy consultation at Chieti Hospital

15th April
MOC-DEXA at Ortona Hospital

16th April
2nd Visit to Oncology Clinic at Chieti Hospital. Histology received confirming no chemotherapy is required. Receive prescriptions for Letrozolo and D base.

23rd April
First consultation for radiotherapy at Pescara Hospital

11th May
Test run and tattoos in preparation for radiotherapy at Pescara Hospital

23rd June to 23rd July
Radiotherapy at Pescara Hospital

8th October
Blood Tests for Integrated Medicine programme (also 6-month check)

12th October
First appointment with Integrated Medicine Ortona Hospital (begin one week of monitoring)

21st October
Begin Integrated Medicine Programme with personal nutrition & exercise plan, online support, regular checks and acupuncture.

27th October
Upper body ultrasound at private hospital near Chieti (preparation for 6-month oncology check)

10th November
6-month check at Oncology Clinic, Chieti Hospital

ABOUT THE AUTHOR

Mair Stratton lives in the Abruzzo region of Italy with her husband and several 'supposed to be feral' cats. Before leaving the UK to embrace the dolce vita she worked a sponsorship consultant in sports and the arts, and as an Event Director. Since swapping the daily commute into London for a view of the Apennine Mountains, she has faced some significant challenges. Grappling with the complexities of the Italian language is one. Choosing the ultimate ice cream flavour is another. She distracts herself by writing. She is currently writing her third book.

Printed in Great Britain
by Amazon

76135878R00132